BRAZIL
CARNIVAL
OF THE
OPPRESSED

LULA AND THE
BRAZILIAN
WORKERS' PARTY

**Sue Branford
& Bernardo Kucinski**

1.00

The Latin America Bureau is an independent research and publishing organisation. It works to broaden public understanding of human rights and social and economic injustice in Latin America and the Caribbean.

First published in the UK in 1995 by the Latin America Bureau (Research and Action) Ltd, 1 Amwell Street, London EC1R 1UL

© Sue Branford and Bernardo Kucinski

A CIP catalogue record for the book is available from the British Library
ISBN 0 906156 99 8

Editor: Duncan Green
Cover design: Andy Dark
Photos: Tony Samphier
Map: Michael Green

Printed by Russell Press, Nottingham NG7 3HJ
Trade distribution in UK by Central Books, 99 Wallis Road, London E9 5LN
Distribution in North America by Monthly Review Press, 122 West 27th Street, New York, NY 10001

Contents

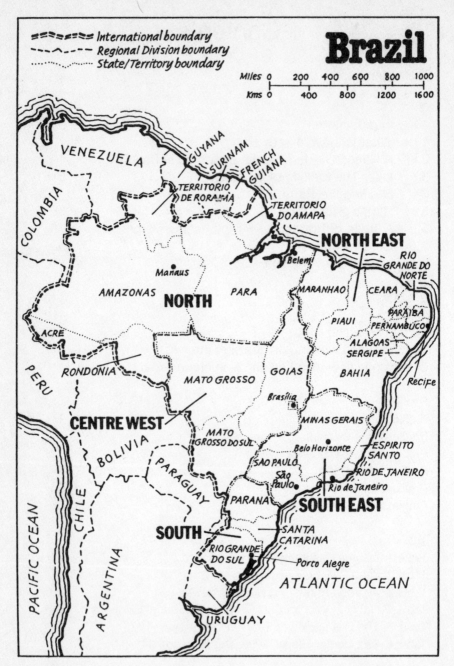

Brazil

International boundary
Regional Division boundary
State/Territory boundary

Miles 0 200 400 600 800 1000
Kms 0 400 800 1200 1600

VENEZUELA

GUYANA

SURINAM

FRENCH GUIANA

COLOMBIA

TERRITORIO DE RORAIMA

TERRITORIO DO AMAPA

NORTH EAST

Belem

RIO GRANDE DO NORTE

Manaus

AMAZONAS

NORTH

PARA

MARANHAO

CEARA

PIAUI

PARAIBA

PERNAMBUCO

ACRE

ALAGOAS

SERGIPE

RONDONIA

MATO GROSSO

GOIAS

BAHIA

Recife

PERU

Brasília

CENTRE WEST

BOLIVIA

MATO GROSSO DO SUL

MINAS GERAIS

Belo Horizonte

ESPIRITO SANTO

PARAGUAY

SAO PAULO

São Paulo

RIO DE JANEIRO

PARANA

Rio de Janeiro

SOUTH EAST

CHILE

SOUTH

SANTA CATARINA

RIO GRANDE DO SUL

Porto Alegre

ARGENTINA

ATLANTIC OCEAN

PACIFIC OCEAN

URUGUAY

IV

Glossary

ABC	Industrial belt around São Paulo, named after the initials of its three main towns, Santo André, São Bernardo and São Caetano
ABCD	ABC region, plus Diadema
ALN	*Ação de Libertação Nacional* National Liberation Action, one of Brazil's first urban guerrilla movements, set up by Carlos Marighella in the late 1960s
Articulação	Tendency set up within PT by 113 trade union leaders and others to combat small left-wing groups. Dominant in internal party affairs from its foundation in 1983 to its division in 1993.
bóias frias	Day workers on large farms, living in nearby towns
caravanas	Lula's long fact-finding trips throughout Brazil, aimed at promoting the PT and getting to know the country
CEB	*Comunidade Eclesial de Base* base Christian community of the Roman Catholic Church
coletivo	a group created around a progressive issue such as women's or gay rights
CUT	*Central Única dos Trabalhadores* Left-wing trade union federation, set up in 1983 with PT support
Cruzado plan	Failed economic stabilisation plan launched in 1986 by President José Sarney
Força Sindical	Second largest trade union federation, (anti-PT)
Frente Nacional de Prefeitos	National Front of Mayors. Set up by PT and other parties to lobby for disbursement of funds from state and federal governments

Frente Brasil Popular	Brazil Popular Front. A left-wing coalition that backed Lula in the 1989 election
MST	*Movimento dos Sem-Terra* Landless Peasant Movement
Opção de Esquerda	Left-wing group that emerged from *Articulação* after 1993 split
pardo	mixed-race Brazilian
PCB	*Partido Comunista Brasileiro* Brazilian Communist Party (pro-Soviet)
PCBR	*Partido Comunista Brasileiro Revolucionário* Brazilian Revolutionary Communist Party
PC do B	*Partido Comunista do Brasil* Communist Party of Brazil (pro-China)
pelego	pejorative term for pro-company union leader
petista	Workers' Party activist
PFL	*Partido da Frente Liberal* Liberal Front Party, right-wing member of Cardoso's ruling coalition
PMDB	*Partido do Movimento Democrático Brasileiro* Party of the Brazilian Democratic Movement Largest centre party
policlínicas	local health centres set up by PT administration in Santos
PPS	*Partido Popular Socialista* Popular Socialist Party, tiny renamed former communist party that took part in 1989 election

PSB	*Partido Socialista Brasileiro* Brazilian Socialist Party, not member of Socialist International
PSDB	*Partido da Social-Democracia Brasileira* Brazilian Social Democratic Party, centre-left party of current president Fernando Henrique Cardoso
PT	*Partido dos Trabalhadores* Workers' Party
Real	New currency introduced in July 1994 by then Finance Minister Fernando Henrique Cardoso
Real plan	Stabilisation programme introduced by Cardoso which won him the 1994 election by cutting inflation from 50% to 2% a month
Tribunal Municipal de Contas	Appointed body of five highly-paid judges that checks the São Paulo municipal accounts
UDR	*União Democrática Ruralista* Democratic Rural Union. Extremely right- wing landowners' organisation.
Unidade na Luta	Unity in Struggle. Centre group of *Articulação* after 1993 split

Epigraph

In all countries there are people, in numbers large and small, who are moved by a vision of a new social order in which democracy, egalitarianism and co-operation — the essential values of Socialism — would be the prevailing principles of social organisation. It is in the growth in their numbers and in the success of their struggles that lies the best hope for human kind.

Ralph Miliband, in *Socialism for a Sceptical Age*

Introduction

In May 1994, José Sarney, a former president and bitter opponent of the Workers' Party, commented, 'There's no human force in the world that can stop Lula from winning these elections.' Though most *petistas*, as supporters of the Workers' Party (*Partido dos Trabalhadores*, PT) are called, reserve a special scorn for Sarney, an old ally of the military who emerged in 1985 as Brazil's first civilian president for 21 years, they almost all agreed with him. Luís Inácio da Silva, universally known as Lula, the charismatic union leader who in the late 1970s became a household name for the courageous way in which he led the wave of strikes that swept through the factories of Brazil's largest city, São Paulo, seemed unstoppable.

As centre and right-wing political parties floundered, Lula forged ahead in the opinion polls. His campaign message that, before anything else, Brazil had to tackle the severe social crisis that was tearing the country apart, seemed to respond to the mood of the country. Lula, the self-educated trade unionist, would be elected president in the elections in October 1994, at the head of a powerful front of left-wing forces, including trade unions, mass-based movements, ecological activists and human rights campaigners. With an overtly socialist programme, the new government would be the most important development in left-wing politics in Latin America since the victory of the Sandinistas in Nicaragua in 1979.

It was not to be. Scared into action by the prospect of a PT victory, the right and the centre joined forces. With the enthusiastic collaboration of the Itamar Franco government, a scheme was worked out for catapulting into the presidency, not an old-style populist politician who the coalition knew would be unacceptable to the country, but a renowned intellectual, a committed centre-left politician who, thirty years earlier, had been a vehement opponent of the military regime. The reasoning behind the new strategy was that it was only from the snake's venom that one could produce the serum for the snake's bite. The new candidate, Fernando Henrique Cardoso, was the antidote to Lula.

An economic stabilisation plan was rejigged. The introduction of a new currency, the *Real*, was deliberately brought forward to have maximum political effect. Inflation dropped from a punitive 50 per cent a month to just two or three per cent. The mood of the country changed almost overnight. According to Eduardo Gianetti da Fonseca, a social psychologist at the University of São Paulo, 'One of the most striking characteristics of

3

the Brazilian people is the way in which it experiences abrupt changes in social expectations. We move rapidly from deep pessimism to exaggerated optimism and vice-versa.'

Suddenly Lula's strongly ethical message, which demanded sacrifices from the better-off in the name of the integration into society of the millions of 'excluded' Brazilians, seemed outdated. A new and easier solution was on offer – rapid economic development and Brazil's successful integration into the world market. The new tone was set by economists like Paulo Rabello de Castro, who offered what amounted to a technical quick fix for Brazil's long political and social crisis, 'We are like a transatlantic liner whose course is set in the direction of stabilisation and globalisation. There is no going back for this ship.'

The hastily assembled strategy worked. On 3 October, Fernando Henrique Cardoso was elected comfortably in the first round, taking 54 per cent of the vote, compared to just 27 per cent for Lula.

Yet the elections were not a complete disaster for the PT, which significantly increased its presence in Congress and elected for the first time two state governors. The party is already running more than fifty towns, including four state capitals. All this gives it ample scope to put into practice its novel and imaginative ideas about direct democracy, which have made the party into the largest and most exciting laboratory of left-wing politics in the world.

Most *petistas* are still confident that their time will come, perhaps in the not too distant future. As the Mexican financial crisis of early 1995 showed, neoliberalism has not provided Latin America with the panacea for its development problems that Cardoso suggested throughout his electoral campaign. The mood in Brazil in early 1995 is still confident as, in the old populist tradition of finding saviours for the country's dilemmas, Cardoso is being projected as the 'great intellectual' who will lead Brazil into a new era of growth and prosperity.

Even the highly respected news magazine, *Veja*, fed the myth, 'Never have we had in the presidency such an illustrious politician as Cardoso, a man who has found his way through at least 10,000 books. If he cannot overcome our problems, where will we find anyone better prepared to do so?' As the optimism inevitably fades, many Brazilians may be receptive once again to the PT's consistent message that the country can only make real progress, which means improving the living standards of all Brazilians, through collective mobilisation.

None of this means that the PT believes it has the whole answer. As Brazil is sucked into a globalised world economy, *petistas* are debating with increasing urgency the future of socialism. What is the role of the state in today's world? How can new alliances be formed, involving trade unionists, peasant families, consumers, ecologists and gay rights activists, to face up to the ever-increasing power of multinational companies? How can Brazil deal with integration on the world market, while protecting its domestic market? How does Brazil achieve modernisation that 'includes' the forty million Brazilians left outside, rather than the kind of modernisation that 'excludes', as is happening in so much of Latin America?

As we show in this book, the PT's history makes it ideally suited to find answers to these questions. *Veja*, not known for its sympathies towards the PT, highlights its main strength: 'The PT has something that the other parties seriously lack – life. In the PT, you will find debate, contradictions, self-sacrificing militants, new ideas. Unlike the other parties, it is not made up of a handful of party bosses and paid electoral agents.'

1
What is the Workers' Party?

The PT has many unusual, even conflicting, characteristics. Although, like the British Labour Party, it was founded by union leaders, it has never had formal institutional links with the unions. Nor have the unions ever controlled it, or even funded it. To remain a broadly-based party the PT has allowed other social groups, such as landless peasant families and state employees, a large say in running the party. Its militants are active in most mass-based movements in Brazil, and lead many of them, but these movements have no formal place in the party structure and frequently clash with municipal governments run by the PT. The party does not have predetermined ideological positions on anything, except for a vague commitment to socialism. It does not even insist that its activists have a party card, nor does it have a clear party doctrine or strict rules for entry. Most *petistas* have never actually joined the party and do not pay party fees. The US sociologist Margaret E. Keck described her influential book on the PT as 'the study of an anomaly'.

The PT resembles Solidarity in Poland in its close links to the Catholic Church, but whereas in Poland the Catholic Church is extremely conservative, with no great democratic tradition or practice, in Brazil it is progressive. Liberation theology, particularly the concept of the base Christian community (CEB), was an important influence in the formation of the party. Despite this, the PT is the only party in Brazil that has ever dared to challenge Catholic dogma. It deals with abortion as a social, rather than an ethical question, and believes that homosexuals should be treated like everyone else. It is a party of Marxists, but not a Marxist party. It operates as a mass party in the public arena, but it is structured as a quasi-Leninist party, run by an executive committee and full-time paid militants, each responsible for a different political, cultural or social activity. Is the PT an anachronistic product of Brazil's belated industrialisation, or is it the forerunner of an altogether new kind of political organisation? Is it a party at all or a social movement?

The PT could be tentatively defined as an 'open' party, just as there are 'open' works of art, where new participants are not only welcomed, but by joining change the final product. This happened when the party was first created. Several left-wing groups joined, each hoping to shape it according to its view, but none succeeded entirely. The PT began, instead, a process of endless change, constantly adapting to the demands of new members. The first mass party ever to exist in Brazil, it attracted both the traditional mass-based movements that fight for material gains and the popular movements concerned with the 'new issues' such as environment, culture and sexuality (see profile, page 16). Whereas western political parties have, on the whole, failed to respond to such new issues, the PT represents these demands institutionally. In this sense, it has become a post-modern political organisation without parallel anywhere in the world.

* * *

To understand this 'open' party, we need to know what it is that keeps the *petistas* together, besides a vague adherence to socialism. It is not a particular definition of socialism, far less a specific recipe on how to achieve it, but an ethos, an attitude towards society and political involvement that combines radicalism, self-denial and moral outrage. This is the common denominator of all *petistas*, be they intellectuals, workers, Catholics, agnostic activists, members of the Landless Peasant Movement or organisers of women's rights groups. If an activist within a particular movement or community is a radical and does not act out of self-interest, then he or she will probably be a *petista*. This attitude is in itself an act of defiance against the dominant traits in Brazil's political culture: conciliation, tolerance and mutual self-interest. The *petista* ethos, associated with the party since its creation, has become the party's indelible trademark. It explains the PT's inability to act opportunistically, its failure to seize short-term political gains and its resistance to political horse-trading. In the eyes of its supporters, *petismo* stands for morality in politics. Many of the PT's adversaries, however, are irritated by what they see as an arrogant and self-righteous attitude of moral superiority.

This ethos is traced back by social scientists to the base Christian communities and other mass-based movements that mushroomed in Brazil in the 1970s. There were hundreds of small organisations, mostly formed by migrants who came to the big cities from the impoverished north-east. The 80,000 CEBs alone had an estimated membership of two million. The migrants had to build their lives in the cities in very difficult conditions. With little help from the authorities, they had to build themselves a shack, get a job and sort out the other problems of everyday life.

These were the elements that in the past had underpinned populism in Brazil and elsewhere in Latin America. Though not really committed to migrant families, the typical populist leader built up his prestige and his electoral strength by providing them with public services. But Brazil in the 1970s was being ruled by the military, which harshly repressed all kinds of

8

political activity, including populism. Nor could the newcomers get help from the clandestine left-wing parties, which had suffered a series of ideological and military defeats.

Into this vacuum stepped the progressive wing of the Catholic Church, which had been encouraged by the 'preferential option for the poor' made by Latin American bishops at the Medellín Conference in 1968. With the Church's backing, the migrants could meet and work out how to satisfy their basic needs – how to bring water into their community, how to get the council to create a new bus route to take them to work, how to run self-help schemes for building more permanent homes. In this way, they developed the qualities of self-reliance and solidarity and learned how to take control of their own lives, building their own identity through the process of organising themselves. In so doing, they began to believe that they could challenge the system that was making their lives so difficult. Soon, the growth of mass-based movements reached the factories, giving birth to a new kind of union movement. 'New unionism', driven by the same values, led eventually to the formation of a new political party, the PT. These values were captured in the most popular protest song of the time, Geraldo Vandré's *Caminhando*, banned by the military, which became the anthem of the base Christian communities. In the words of the chorus:

Vem, vamos embora que esperar não é fazer;
Quem sabe faz a hora, não espera acontecer...

Come, let's go, for waiting is not doing,
Let's make the moment, not wait for it to happen...

Despite tough anti-labour legislation and close police surveillance, a new breed of leaders emerged to head 'new unionism', which was particularly strong in the industrial belt around São Paulo known as the ABC region after the names of the main towns, Santo André, São Bernardo and São Caetano. This region was growing rapidly as many multinational companies, particularly car manufacturers, set up new factories there, becoming a magnet for migrants from the impoverished north-east attracted south in search of jobs. They brought with them the base Christian community ideas of self-organisation, participation and liberation.

The new leadership was both pragmatic and committed, more concerned with workers' well-being than with defining itself politically. Unlike other activists who were trying to organise workers outside the official union structure, the 'new unionists' aimed to take over the unions and make them truly independent, outside the control of both the government and political groups, including left-wing parties. For them, industrial action was not an instrument for furthering the interests of any political party, but for increasing their members' share in the wealth of the country. They combined determination with an ability to negotiate.

Luis Inácio da Silva, so widely known as Lula that he had eventually to change his name by deed poll to Luís Inácio Lula da Silva so that voters would recognise him on the ballot paper, was the most prominent leader of the 'new unionism'. The story of his early life and growing political awareness is told in chapter 3. When he led the first strike in São Paulo in 1978, Lula was a union leader with scant education or culture but an acute understanding of the predicament of industrial workers. Unlike the early generation of union leaders, who paid lip service to nationalism, he saw Brazilian companies as no better than foreign ones. If anything, he thought that multinationals treated their workers somewhat better.

'New unionism' challenged a traditional left-wing strategy, frequently adopted by the Brazilian Communist Party (PCB). Being proscribed for much of its existence in Brazil, the Communist Party had developed a manipulative attitude towards unions, using them for its own political ends. This meant persuading the union to accept populist schemes or even state control, whenever this was seen to be in the party's interest.

'New unionism', in contrast, demanded full union freedom and the right to negotiate collective work contracts as in other capitalist economies. The new union leaders attacked the *pelegos*, literally the cowhide that horsemen put underneath the saddle to stop it rubbing a sore patch on the horse's skin. Used figuratively, it denotes union officials who play the employers' game. They were also critical of the trade union tax, equivalent to one day's wages per year, which was collected by the labour ministry from all employees and then distributed to different unions. The tax allowed unions to survive, irrespective of the support they had among the workforce, and encouraged corruption and the manipulation of the unions by government. 'New unionism' wanted to abolish the tax and make the unions completely independent of the state. Only union leaders completely confident of support from their members could have made such a proposal.

Lula's work as a trade unionist led him to two basic conclusions: workers had to be autonomous, in control of their own destinies, and strikes, even if successful, would never be enough to change the fundamental predicament faced by workers in a country where social and labour demands were treated, ultimately, as criminal acts of subversion. These views prompted his decision to set up a new political party:

I believe that it is possible that we workers will, in the very near future, be able to create from below our own political party, with the participation, eventually, not only of workers, but of all those who align themselves with the principles of the working class.
Lula, May 1978

I've come to believe that workers cannot simply cast their votes at election time for people who pretend to be on the side of workers, at times offering them favours in exchange for votes. I realize that workers have to organise themselves politically.
Lula, April 1980

The decision by Lula and the other 'new unionists' to found their own party split the left, but the idea prospered and the PT was formally founded in 1980, standing in elections for the first time in 1982. Chapter 4 tells the story of the party's formation and its astonishing growth over the following decade.

* * *

At least until late 1994, the PT was the main political beneficiary of Brazil's deepening crisis, but this in turn led to a crisis of expectations. The party has been like a galaxy expanding at such a speed that it has left much empty space behind it. In only fifteen years, the PT has become one of the largest parties in Brazil and a serious contender for power, but in this process, as we shall see, it has been defeated at its very birthplace and former stronghold, the ABC industrial belt around São Paulo. It has also failed to incorporate into its daily life many young voters as they come onto the political stage. To the concern of some veteran members, including Lula, it is starting to behave more and more like a conventional parliamentary party.

Despite this, the PT's main source of strength continues to lie in its links with the union movement. Unlike the situation in most industrialised countries, unions are still remarkably powerful in Brazil and their support is often decisive. It is not just that about twenty per cent of the sixty million workforce is unionised. Unions also have money, structure, organisation and cadres and are particularly strong in the engineering, banking and state sectors. The party has very strong links with the largest union federation, the CUT (*Central Única dos Trabalhadores*), which was created in August 1983 by union workers who supported the PT. It already has 4.5 million paid up members, including most of the country's most militant union leaders. Like the PT, the CUT encourages self-organisation and independence from both the government and political parties. It is a political machine of considerable weight, publishing newspapers and magazines, and running several research institutes and a couple of colleges for union leaders. The second largest union federation in Brazil, *Força Sindical*, spends most of its time fighting the CUT and the PT. Even though it enjoys favourable press coverage and generous government support, it only has about 850,000 paid-up members and represents just a few major unions, mostly in backward sectors of the economy. There are two other union federations, one of them representing rural workers.

Along with the Catholic Church and, to a much lesser extent, the Communist Party of Brazil (PC do B), the PT has considerable influence over a variety of mass-based movements. The most important is the Landless Peasant Movement (MST), which organises various acts of civil disobedience, particularly land occupations, to force the government to expropriate large estates and distribute them to the poor. There are an estimated 4.8 million peasant families without land in Brazil. Because many of them feel extremely frustrated at being denied a small plot of land in a country with so many huge and unproductive estates, this movement is one of the most militant organisations in Brazil. The reaction from landlords has been ferocious, and land invasions frequently lead to violence and deaths.

The Catholic Church exerts great influence over the MST, particularly through its Pastoral Land Commission, and the Church gives the movement its missionary spirit of self-sacrifice and martyrdom. Under the leadership of a radical Catholic priest, Father Ticão, the Church is also active in the homeless movement in the vast, poor settlements to the east of the city of São Paulo. With 18,000 members, it is the largest of its kind in the world. Father Ticão also runs a nationwide homeless movement. The Catholic Church is directly involved in other mass-based movements, too, through other Pastoral Commissions. Many leaders in these mass-based movements are simultaneously activists in the PT. The relationship between party and movements is close; demands put forward by mass-based movements are almost automatically incorporated into the party's programme.

* * *

The PT is a unique organisation in Brazilian politics. It has militants, regular meetings, and a permanently functioning structure that operates at local, regional and national level. It has about 600,000 militants distributed between 2,304 regional directorates, as its local groups are known. Most other parties do not have any significant structure, few militants, and function only at election time. For its militants, the PT is more than just a party; it is a lifestyle, a meeting point, a culture; the PT is the 'let's party party', as many activists acknowledge.

At the outset, the PT set up two mechanisms to guarantee internal party democracy. One was the 'pre-convention'. Before national party conventions, held each year, the PT organises a large number of preliminary meetings at all levels – municipal, regional and national – and makes sure that the views expressed at these meetings are taken fully into account at the national convention. Though cumbersome, these 'pre-conventions' ensure a level of internal democracy unprecedented in Brazilian politics.

The second, complementary mechanism is the so-called 'party nucleus', seen as a way of allowing ordinary members to express their political views and to have a say in running the party. Though superficially akin to the Leninist cell of traditional leftist parties, the nucleus has, in fact, more affinity with the structure of the base Christian community. Nuclei can be organised at work, in the neighbourhood, or in a social movement. The idea is to maximise the participation of each PT member and to help members develop their political awareness.

Reacting against the much-hated concept of 'democratic centralism', which had been repeatedly used in 'Stalinist' parties to justify internal repression, the founding members of the new party were insistent that few constraints should be placed on the behaviour of members. One of the party's first documents declared:

> A party that wishes to create a socialist and democratic society must itself be a democratic organisation, respecting the rights of minorities to diverge and to dissent, but with the understanding that only individuals (and not organisations) can affiliate to the party.

In practice, this meant that small clandestine left-wing political groups were initially allowed to operate quite freely within the party, even though they admitted that they were really a party within the party, with their own financial structure, papers and closed meetings. 'It is not for us, but for the police, to control political organisations', said Lula. After decades of dictatorship, the party wanted to show solidarity with all who had suffered political repression. Although political realities subsequently forced the PT to restrict the activities of these tendencies, the party is still proud of the way it acted as a refuge for political activists.

Perhaps because the rank-and-file is so strong, the party has hundreds of regional or local publications but has failed to develop an important national journal. In contrast with classic communist parties, the PT has never run a national newspaper of importance. The first attempt, *Jornal dos Trabalhadores*, launched in 1982, closed down. A second attempt, *Brasil Agora*, launched in 1991, still exists but has a circulation of less than 20,000. As a result, most of the party's ideological debate with other political organisations takes place in the mainstream newspaper, *Folha de S.Paulo*. The party also publishes a sort of official gazette, *Boletim Nacional*, and *Teoria e Debate*, a theoretical magazine with about 15,000 subscribers, which reflects the political debates taking place among the party's cadres.

* * *

The party's main deliberative body is its annual National Meeting, for which delegates are elected directly by each of the local groups, with a minimum of thirty per cent of seats reserved for women. Candidates in elections must be nominated by a certain number of local groups and then endorsed by the relevant directorates. In 1991 the National Meeting was given a new status, becoming the PT's First Congress.

The party structure has strong roots in the mass-based organisations. Any *coletivo*, as a group created around a progressive issue is called, has almost automatic legitimacy within the party. There are dozens of *coletivos*: women's rights groups, gay groups, artists' groups and so on. In the early days, there were serious sectarian conflicts between party activists and PT-run local councils, but today sectarianism has largely disappeared. Intellectuals and activists who do not belong to any particular tendency within the party can still feel left out, but can play a role in running the numerous local governments now under PT control. In Luiza Erundina's government in São Paulo, Paul Singer, a highly respected economist, became planning secretary, Marilena Chauí, a university philosophy professor, was culture secretary, and Paulo Freire, the renowned educationalist, was appointed education secretary.

Not all of the so-called minority groups are happy with what the party is doing for them. Gay activists believe that the party could be doing more to combat homophobia in the labour movement; women believe that they are still discriminated against in the party. Benedita da Silva, Brazil's first black senator (see profile, page 32), was one of the prime movers in getting the party to accept, in principle, that thirty per cent of executive positions should be allocated to women. Even so, she believes that not enough has changed, 'Women are extremely important at the base of the party. They have had an absolutely fundamental role in getting society to engage in social questions. But they still face a lot of discrimination and prejudice, both in society as a whole and inside the party. Women are still controlled – by their fathers, their husbands, their partners. It's very difficult, but over the last two decades women have shown that they can get involved in politics in their own way, without losing their tenderness.'

Many *petista* women believe that the party is still controlled by men. This, they say, is bad for the PT. Men are selected as party candidates in elections, when, they say, there are stronger women candidates. Telma de Souza, former mayor of Santos and now federal deputy, explains, 'Imagine, we only managed to get two women adopted by the party to run in the elections for federal deputy. If it's like this in São Paulo, you can imagine what it's like in the rest of the country. What worries me is that if we don't take great care, we're going to find that we have fewer and fewer women, fewer and fewer blacks, fewer and fewer of the other minorities occupying key jobs within the party. That is very dangerous for a party like the PT that claims to be a mass movement.' Despite such complaints, most women admit that the situation is even worse in the other parties.

14

* * *

Between national meetings the party is run by the 86 members of the National Directorate. The Directorate meets regularly, an expensive exercise in party democracy in a country as huge as Brazil, and one not undertaken by any other party. The party spends hours talking about every issue. The discussions are often disorganised and proposals can be impractical, but in a country with so little previous experience of democracy, most *petistas* feel proud of the real freedom of expression they enjoy.

Before an alliance is made in Congress or elsewhere, it has to be discussed at length by the National Directorate. All members of Congress have to give the party one third of their salaries. The principle of accountability is also firmly established. Once a policy is adopted, it must be supported by the PT's members elected to office. This, in itself, is a novelty in a country where elected politicians feel accountable to no one, least of all the voters who elected them or the party to which they formally belong. But the policy has caused some controversy within the PT, largely because of the rigid wording of some of the party's resolutions. The mainstream press has criticised the whole procedure for being dogmatic and sectarian, but not infrequently the scheme has helped strengthen the party, as was the case of the Directorate's decision, initially unpopular among the general public, not to allow PT members to vote for Tancredo Neves at the electoral college in 1985 (see chapter 5).

The PT also faced a barrage of criticism from the mainstream press for its fierce opposition first to Congress drawing up the country's new constitution in 1988 and later to Congress carrying out a revision of this constitution, a decision which earned its deputies the nickname of 'Brazil's contras' in the mainstream press. On both occasions, the PT argued that Congress did not have the legitimacy to carry out these tasks as it was not sufficiently representative of the wide range of groups and interests in society. Though its stance was not popular at the time among the general public, the subsequent budget scandal, which implicated a majority of the members of Congress in a corruption network, meant that the party eventually gained widespread respect for its position.

Profile: Guilherme

With his Lula T-shirt cut down to skimpy vest size, Guilherme looks like a seasoned PT *militante*. He is also one of the PT's leading gay rights activists. Though, as he says, there is a thriving gay scene in Brazil's cities, homosexuality remains taboo. Gays who admit to their sexuality face discrimination in employment and violence on the streets. It is estimated that about 1,200 gay people have been murdered over the last decade because of their sexual orientation. Guilherme himself knew one local councillor who, after he had 'come out' about his sexuality, lost his job in government and was then kidnapped and killed.

According to Guilherme, AIDS has increased discrimination. 'Despite all the evidence to the contrary, some Brazilian doctors still say that it is an illness that just affects the gay community,' he says. 'This has encouraged the rise of neo-Nazi groups that target gays and lesbians.' Guilherme says the PT is the only party that is trying to do something for the gay community. According to a PT leaflet published in 1994 by the party's gay and lesbian committee, 'It is in the PT that, for the first time in Brazilian history, gays and lesbians have won the freedom to organise themselves.'

Even so, Guilherme believes that the PT is still doing too little. 'I want more action in the trade unions,' he says. 'Most of them simply don't have any position on the issue and there is still a lot of discrimination in the labour movement.' As yet, Brazilians do not have the constitutional right to choose freely their own sexual orientation. Guilherme supports the party's proposal for a human rights comission. 'That could be a big step towards passing legislation that defends the rights, not only of the gay community, but of the disabled.'

But the PT has to tread carefully. Even the cautiously worded statement in the PT's 1994 manifesto, which defended the right of citizens not to suffer discrimination because of their sexuality, was ferociously attacked by a hostile press.

(Interview by Tony Samphier)

Profile: Maria Osmarina Silva de Souza

With her striking looks and ready smile, Marina, as she is widely known, is the latest PT sensation. Born into a poor family of rubber-tappers in the Amazon state of Acre, she learnt to read and write when she was 16 years old, and, after a meteoric political career, was elected to an eight-year term as senator in October 1994. She and Benedita da Silva are the first PT women to have become senators.

Marina's life seems like a fairy tale. In February 1958 she was born in a hut made out of the trunks of palm trees and standing on poles to protect it from the seasonal river floods, on an isolated rubber plantation 70km from Rio Branco, the capital of Acre. The rubber-tappers and their families received little medical assistance, for a lengthy river journey separated them from the outside world. Marina's parents had eleven children but, without medical assistance, three died as babies. Marina recalls, 'I saw electric light for the first time when I was taken by river to Rio Branco to receive treatment for poisoning caused by remedies for worms. I still remember the amazement I felt seeing a Christmas tree decorated with fairy lights.'

When she was about five, her family moved to the town of Manaus on the Amazon river, where they set up a small store. But the shop went bankrupt in five months, and they all travelled by boat, sleeping in hammocks, to the mouth of the river. There they planted cassava to make manioc flour, but again the initiative failed. Marina's father got in touch with the owner of the rubber plantation back in Acre, and he agreed to pay for them to go back, provided that the family paid off the debt by producing extra rubber. Still just ten years old, Marina used to get up at five in the morning every day of the week, to make the 14km trek through the forest with her father and elder sister, first to slit the trunks of the rubber trees and then to collect the latex. They paid off the debt. Like other members of her family, Marina was often ill, suffering from five attacks of malaria and two bouts of hepatitis.

When Marina was 15 years old, two of her sisters died within a fortnight, one from malaria and the other from measles. Six months later her mother died from a stroke. She begged her father to let her go to Rio Branco to realise her two dreams; to study and to become a nun. Marina said later, 'It was the most important moment of my life. My father said yes and I left the plantation. I first stepped into a school when I was 16 years old.'

Despite her late start, Marina proved an excellent student. By the time she was 26, she had graduated in history at the University of Acre, financing her studies by working as a maid. By then she had given up the idea of being a nun, 'I realised that I would have to repress all my sexuality and that wasn't the right option for me', and had married. Partly through her participation in base Christian communities, she became politicised. She took part in *empates*, actions of civil resistance, organised by the renowned rubber-tapper, Chico Mendes, during which whole communities of rubber-tappers stopped the tractors sent in by cattle-ranchers to clear the forest. She helped Chico Mendes set up a local branch of the CUT, the powerful trade union body with close links to the PT.

Her husband disapproved of her growing involvement in politics, and eventually they separated. Marina says that it was a difficult decision for her, because by then she had two children and was still deeply religious. She eventually married again and had two more children. In 1988, a year after Chico Mendes was murdered by a cattle-rancher, she was elected to the municipal council. With her dark skin and long, curly black hair, Marina, like so many of the region's other inhabitants, is of mixed ethnic origins, largely Afro-indian. In 1990, she was elected state deputy, obtaining the largest number of votes ever recorded in Acre.

She was very active as a deputy, but in 1991 was taken seriously ill. PT friends helped fly her down to São Paulo, but no doctor could discover what was wrong with her. She recalls, 'I felt a strange taste on my tongue, as if I had put a coin in my mouth. I told everyone that I was suffering from metal poisoning, but the medical tests showed nothing.' Eventually Marina found a specialist in the field who confirmed her suspicions. The specialist believes that her heavy metal contamination was caused by the strong medicine she received for malaria attacks when she still lived in the forest. She has responded to treatment, but has to be very careful what she eats, avoiding all processed foods.

In the 1994 elections, she received the most votes in Acre. She puts her goals for the next eight years in simple terms, 'To fight for the excluded and to work for the ecologically-sustainable development of the Amazon'. One rubber-tapper comments, 'Chico Mendes must be happy'.

18

2
A Nation Divided:
Social Apartheid in Brazil

Two teenagers were sitting in their car eating cheeseburgers at a MacDonald's drive-in in the capital city, Brasília. To amuse themselves, they were casually tossing potato chips out of the window, as if feeding dogs. Instead, it was street children who were scrabbling on the ground after the food. Other customers watched, laughing.

Cristovam Buarque, a former chancellor of Brasília University who was elected mayor of Brasília in November 1994, is one of the PT's most original thinkers. He began a recent book with a description of this scene, which he had witnessed. It could only happen, he says, because the wealthy youngsters felt nothing in common with the barefooted urchins. The deep divisions in Brazilian society, he believes, are comparable to those in South Africa before it started dismantling apartheid. A wealthy, largely white élite lives in its own world of chauffeur-driven cars, luxury homes protected by heavily-fortified fences and teams of security guards, while the poor, largely black or mulatto mass of the population lives in a world of hunger, overcrowded shacks and drug-related violence. To describe this phenomenon, Buarque coined the phrase 'social apartheid'.

The social divide is evident in many facets of Brazilian life, but most dramatically in the lives of its children. Claúdio, known as *Cacau* ('Cocoa', presumably because of his dark skin), is eleven years old; his brother, Felipe, known as Buiu, is nine. They live in a tiny, one-roomed shack with eight other children and seven adults in the Rocinha shanty town in the south of Rio de Janeiro. At night, they all – siblings, cousins, mother, father, grandmother, aunt and uncle – sleep together in two beds. The shack has no water, save that seeping down the walls and, along with the other huts, gets its electricity from an illegal, improvised connection from an overhead power line.

The two boys get most of their food from the administrators of the shanty town, elected by the local neighbourhood association, in exchange for running errands such as showing visitors around. Unlike his brother, who stopped going to school two years ago, Buiu still goes to primary school, but he finds it boring and wants to give it up. 'When I grow up I want to open a small shop with my mother', he says. But his mother, Ludéia, 48 years old and unemployed, dismisses his dreams, saying that she she will never have the money to start a business. *Cacau* wants to be a farmer, 'I like all kinds of animals – cows, horses, parrots', he explains.

There are other children worse off than any of these. A few miles away from the Rocinha shanty town, in the far smarter areas of Ipanema and Copacabana, live 12-year-old Roberto, known as Pio, and eight-year-old Felipe Francisco, known as Teo. They follow the street markets, held each day in a different street, and survive from the tips they earn by pushing home shopping trolleys for middle-class customers. At night they sleep under viaducts and are constantly sniffing glue, to which they are both addicted. They are the famous 'street kids', as youngsters who have lost all contact with their parents are known. They are undernourished, have frequent attacks of diarrhoea, and suffer from chronic skin complaints, including scabies. Teo hopes to become a lorry driver when he grows up; Pio just wants to become a 'worker, with a proper job'.

The life of rich children could not be more different. Recently the weekly news magazine, *Veja*, gave its readers a taste. In May 1994, Luiz Estevão de Oliveira Neto decided to hold a party at his home in Brasília. Not an ordinary party, because Luiz Estevão is not an ordinary man. He is the owner of the OK group, with an annual turnover of US$200 million from civil construction and the sale of cars and tyres. He has long been notorious in Brasília for his extravagant life style, but he became known throughout Brazil when his name appeared as guarantor to a highly dubious US$5 million loan from Uruguay. One of his close friends, the then President Fernando Collor de Mello, under investigation for corruption, claimed that the loan accounted for the high deposits in his bank account.

Luiz Estevão invited 1,200 people to his party (including Rosane Collor, the wife of the disgraced president, who commented afterwards, 'It was lovely to feel everyone's affection, after so long away'). The decoration, inspired by 19th century Venetian banquet halls, cost US$33,000, of which US$8,000 went to a prestigious decorator, flown in from New York and put up in a five star hotel. The buffet supper, which cost US$35,000, was transported from São Paulo, together with a hundred catering staff, in two lorries and two coaches. The star performer, the singer Lulu Santos, was going to charge US$25,000 for his performance, but agreed to bring down the price to US$15,000 after Luiz Estevão found him another engagement for the following day in Brasília. All this, at a total cost of US$110,000, to commemorate the 15th birthday of his daughter, Ilca. 'Every father tries to provide the best for his daughter, according to his means,' explained the proud father.

* * *

Such anecdotal evidence of an extraordinarily unjust society is amply supported by statistical evidence:

income distribution: According to a recent United Nations report, only one other nation in the world – Botswana – has greater income disparities than Brazil. Table 1 shows that the richest ten per cent of the population absorbs about half the national income, while the poorest ten per cent have to make do with less than one per cent. The inequality continued to grow throughout the 'lost decade' of severe economic crisis in the 1980s.

Table 1   Income Distribution

	1981	1983	1985	1987	1989	1990
Poorest 10%	0.90	0.90	0.70	0.70	0.60	0.80
Poorest 20%	2.70	2.60	2.40	2.20	2.00	2.40
Poorest 50%	13.40	12.60	12.00	11.70	10.40	11.20
Richest 10%	46.60	48.10	48.80	49.00	53.20	49.70
Richest 5%	33.40	34.50	34.10	35.20	39.40	35.80
Richest 1%	13.00	14.00	14.10	14.50	17.30	14.60

Source: IBGE, PNAD

Poverty in Brazil is not only relative but absolute. According to government figures, about 20 million people, out of an economically active population of 62 million, are either unemployed or earn less than the minimum wage of US$70 a month. Including these people's dependants, this means that there are about 70-80 million Brazilians – about half the population – who are too poor to give their children an adequate upbringing. According to some economists, about 32 million of this deprived population suffer from chronic malnutrition.

The marked contrast between the lives of the very poor and the very rich makes Brazilian poverty particularly obscene. A former social welfare minister, Jutahy Magalhães, observes, 'We are at the same time the most developed and the poorest country in Latin America. We export technology and we produce satellites, but we still haven't eliminated illnesses from the Middle Ages.'

child labour: In circumstances in which the physical survival of families is at stake, it is scarcely surprising that children are encouraged from a very young age to contribute to the family income. It is estimated that about eight million young people between 10 and 17 years old go out to work in Brazil. About two million of them are 13 years old or less. These children, found all over the country, do all kinds of work – as office boys and boot-blacks in the cities; picking cotton and cutting sugar cane in the countryside. Some work as child prostitutes.

Though an individual family may find it essential to send children out to work, child labour brings damaging consequences for the working class as a whole. Employers seeking the cheapest available labour often prefer youngsters to adult workers, dragging down wage levels throughout the economy. As Luiz Claúdio de Vasconcelos from the Labour Ministry points out, 'By accepting a wage that is often one third of the amount paid to an adult, youngsters take jobs that would otherwise have gone to heads of households. This sets up a vicious circle. With their parents out of work, even more children are forced to find a job, and then they themselves can't get the training to break out of the poverty trap.'

Street children with virtually no contact with their families have received the bulk of media attention, yet there are relatively few of them. In 1992 one of Rio's leading research institutes, IBASE, conducted a survey at 3am, scouring the streets of Rio and the impoverished and violent satellite towns on the other side of the river Niterói, known collectively as the Baixada Fluminense. Rather to the institute's surprise, they found only 629 children sleeping rough. The vast majority of street children, it seems, though fending for themselves during the day, go home to sleep at night.

land tenure: Land concentration is one of the chief causes of poverty in Brazil, which has never had a real programme of agrarian reform to redistribute the enormous estates set up by the Portuguese empire in the 16th century. After the 1964 coup, agriculture went through a rapid and intensive process of modernisation. The use of pesticides and fertilisers brought sharp increases in productivity, turning Brazil into a leading exporter of soya beans, oranges, coffee, sugar and alcohol. Modernisation created a middle class of farmers, above all in the south, with farms of 10-100 hectares. There was some limited division of land, as large farmers took advantage of the rapid appreciation in land prices to sell off surplus acreage.

Otherwise, the system of land tenure has remained highly concentrated (see Table 2). There are still many huge estates, of 1 million or 1.5 million hectares, while the average size of small farms is just 3.3 hectares, far too little to support a family. With the backing of the Catholic Church, the powerful Landless Peasant Movement (MST) was set up by peasant families cultivating these tiny plots and then spread to include landless families.

Table 2 Land Distribution in Brazil

Area (in hectares)	% of total number of farms	% of total cultivated area	% of total agricultural workforce
less than 10	52.9	2.7	39.9
from 10 to 100	37.1	18.5	39.7
from 100 to 1000	8.9	35.1	16.1
from 1000 to 10,000	0.8	26.8	4.2
over 10,000	0.04	15	0.1
Total	100	100	100

Sources: IBGE, *Censo Agropecuario*, 1985

Modernisation in farming practice has not changed attitudes. The political movement created by large landowners to protect their estates from land invasions by landless peasants, the Democratic Rural Union (UDR), is one of the most reactionary lobbies in Brazil. According to Plínio Sampaio, a leading PT analyst:

UDR members are not backward in their lifestyle. On the contrary, they have the latest imported cars, Arab stallions, high quality cattle, sophisticated radio networks to keep in close contact with each other. But – and it's very strange – they still find it quite normal to repress violently and illegally any challenge to their power. They employ armed gunmen and don't think twice before sending them off to kill a troublesome union leader.

Mechanisation without agrarian reform has accelerated the rural exodus. There are today several million landless families living in shanty towns in the big cities or on the outskirts of rural towns, working as day labourers. These are the so-called *bóias frias* (cold meals) because they take cold rice and beans to the farm with them for their lunch. The men, women and children are contracted on a daily basis for seasonal farmwork; lorries arrive early every morning to take them to the farms. Many are so desperate for work that they are prepared to accept wages far below the level needed to support themselves or their families.

Nowhere are the paradoxes of Brazil's uneven development as clear as in the farming sector. Paulo Schilling, a veteran left-wing campaigner, wrote recently:

> One of the worst moments in my fifty years of militancy took place in Holland. I had been speaking about the serious problem of malnutrition in Brazil at a seminar organised by non-governmental organisations, trade unions and churches. Afterwards, a Dutch trade unionist drove me to a farm just outside Amsterdam. There, in a sophisticated, modern pig sty, enormous pigs were being fed Brazilian soya beans.

racial mix: The social divisions in the country are reinforced by a subtle but effective system of racism. The contribution of black slaves, brought over from Africa, to forging Brazilian nationhood is little appreciated, even in Brazil itself. Brazil received far more African slaves than any other country in the Americas. A census, carried out in 1817, showed that the country was made up at that time of 1.3 million whites and 3.9 million blacks and mulattos, nearly all of them slaves. According to Rubens Rícupero, one of six finance ministers in the Itamar Franco government, the huge influx of slaves helped shape the mentality of the ruling class:

> Even today we tend to give little importance to labour, which is the least expensive factor of production. Human labour is still regarded as something expendable, that can be lost and replaced. This mentality is typical of slavery. If twenty slaves die, there is no need to worry, you can simply buy up the next shipload that comes in from Angola. This attitude of total superiority lies at the root of the extraordinary imbalance in our income distribution.

Nobody knows the true racial make-up of the Brazilian population today. The 1991 population census, in which people were asked to define their own racial category, suggested that the population was composed of 56 per cent whites, 5 per cent blacks, and 39 per cent 'browns' (*pardos*), a vague term which encompasses mulattos. This break-down almost certainly overestimates the white population, as in Brazilian society many people prefer to classify themselves as whiter than they actually are, but even if it were correct, blacks and mulattos would still be heavily under-represented in every powerful institution in the country, from the judiciary to the senior ranks of the armed forces. Only 12 of the 584 seats in the last Congress (1990-94) were filled by non-whites.

24

At the same time, the poor, black sectors of the population are over-represented at the other end of the social spectrum – in the prisons. The close association between being poor, being black and being a criminal acts as a powerful brake on mobility between the classes. It is only if you know that white men with higher education almost never go to prison that you can understand the delight throughout the country when former President Collor's close aide, Paulo César ('PC') Farias, who ran Collor's huge corruption network, was arrested in Thailand and extradited to await trial in a Brazilian prison.

* * *

The severe social crisis, provoked not so much by lack of resources as by the unwillingness of the rich to share their wealth, has spawned widespread violence. Tradesmen in big cities, exasperated at repeated lootings by adolescent boys too young to be sent to prison, have organised death squads to kill them. With more and more youngsters involved in drug-trafficking, boys frequently die in shoot-outs in the battle for territory in big cities. As a result, violence is now the main cause of death among adolescent boys, something found in no other country in the world not at war; official figures show that murder is the cause of six out of ten deaths among 15-18 year old boys. The police admit that at least seventy per cent of the 1,152 youngsters murdered in Rio de Janeiro in 1993 had been killed by death squads.

Kidnappings, too, are becoming common. The victims are no longer just the very rich, who surround themselves with bodyguards, but also moderately wealthy businessmen and their families, who are less well protected and thus more vulnerable.

This violence has exacerbated the system of social apartheid described by Cristovam Buarque. The rich live in bunkers, protected by fortifications and armed guards. Their children, never allowed to travel by bus, underground or even taxi, go everywhere in chauffeur-driven cars. Violence has become the standard topic of conversation among the Brazilian middle class.

* * *

The government and the public authorities have worsened Brazil's social crisis by systematically intervening on the side of the wealthy, even those governments formally committed to improving the lot of the poor. In successive reports, even the World Bank has strongly criticised the Brazilian government for hurting the interests of the poor. According to several PT analysts, the Brazilian state has been 'privatised', that is, taken over by the ruling élite whose interests it protects. It is, above all, in social policy where the harmful effect of state action on the poor can most clearly be seen:

education: In per capita terms Brazil spends about as much on education as South Korea and Taiwan, but it provides much less for ordinary people. Brazil has about 27 million children of obligatory school age (7-14). Each year about ten million slip through the school net; about five million don't register at the beginning of the year, and another five million fail the end of year exams, often through poor attendance. In part, this reflects the heavy pressure on children to go out to work, yet, as the testimony of many children makes clear, primary schools, many of which are poorly run by barely literate, impoverished teachers, fail to appeal to many poor children as something important and relevant in their lives. Many schools lack the bare essentials; a recent survey showed that 75 per cent had no toilet at all, or one that was not working properly.

The education minister during the Itamar Franco government, Murílio Hingel, was well aware of the deficiencies, 'Despite our efforts, primary education is in a complete mess', he admitted frankly. He particularly regretted the failure of so many children to pass the end of year exams, 'It's a tremendous waste of resources. Without so many children having to repeat years, the load on teachers would be far less and the room shortage far less severe.'

As a result of the crisis in education, a large section of Brazil's population can barely read or write. According to official figures, 19 per cent of the adult population is illiterate, but many specialists say that if people were realistically judged on what they call 'functional literacy', meaning the ability to read and write sufficiently well to meet the requirements of daily life, the illiteracy figure would double.

The poor results are scarcely surprising. Only one-third of the educational budget goes to primary education, far less than in most other countries. Much of the rest of the budget is allocated to university education, mainly benefiting the children of the middle classes and the rich. Brazil spends, on average, US$8,804 on each student in a public university. In Germany, the outlay is US$5,900, in Britain, US$5,100, and in Canada, US$3,975. Brazil has a ratio of 6.5 students per lecturer. In Argentina, it is 16; in France, 23.

public health: In many public hospitals there are far more people lying on stretchers in the corridors waiting to be examined than interned in the wards. People frequently die before they have even been seen by a doctor. Almost every day the newspapers carry interviews with exhausted and angry doctors and nurses. Acary Souza Bulle Oliveira, the administrator of Hospital São Paulo in the centre of the city, told a reporter from the *Folha de S.Paulo*, 'Our resources are inadequate, badly administered, improperly used, and distributed according to political criteria. But we can't just blame the people at the top. It's all our fault. I spend the whole day saying "no" to people, because I haven't the resources. But, instead of getting angry, people meekly accept it, saying "Thank you, doctor".' He went on, 'It's like the violence in Rio. As time goes by, you get used to it and find it normal. But it's wrong; I didn't study medicine to do this.'

The low level of service given to the population does not stem primarily from the lack of resources, but from the perverse combination of chronic mismanagement and a distorted order of priorities. According to government figures, the ministry of health spends as much on highly sophisticated medical treatment for 12,000 favoured patients, many of them from the middle and upper classes, as it does on the remaining forty million people in its care.

Many of the most commonplace health problems could easily be prevented by spending on social infrastructure. Though improvements were made in the 1970s and 1980s in the provision of running water and sewerage, no further advances have been made in recent years. Some 69 per cent of the population (105 million people) are not on a mains sewerage system and 33 per cent (50 million people) have no running water. About 80 per cent of the people going to casualty departments in Brazil's public hospitals are suffering from illnesses caused by poor sanitary conditions.

taxation: The government's built-in bias towards the rich is most clearly evident in the tax system. According to a recent study by Brazil's department of inland revenue, Brazil's tax system is unique. In industrialised countries the highest rate of tax is charged on unearned income – on average, 38 per cent; in Brazil, the figure is just eight per cent. In contrast, Brazil charges a heavy tax on consumption – twenty per cent of the final retail price, compared with five per cent in the USA and Japan. Another study showed that, if all taxes on food were included, as much as one third of the price of basic foodstuffs goes to the government in tax revenue. This is extraordinary in a country where so many people do not have enough to eat.

Brazil's tax system has made it easy for successful businessmen to accumulate huge personal fortunes, quite disproportionate to the value of their companies. According to a Brazilian economist, Ricardo Semler, 'Bill Gates, the richest man in the USA, has a personal fortune of US$4bn, while his company is worth US$30 billion. Sam Walton is worth US$3 billion, and his company US$54 billion. In Brazil, it is different. Roberto Marinho, who owns the Globo media empire, often boasts that he is included in *Forbes* magazine as one of the richest people in the world, with his fortune of US$1billion. But his company is worth only half of this. It's the same with the other thirty wealthiest people in Brazil, and some of them pay no income tax at all.'

* * *

In one of the most remarkable and unreported social revolutions ever to have occurred in Brazilian society, women have been softening the impact of the social crisis on their lives by taking hold of the one power they alone control – the power of reproduction. According to George Martine, 'Brazil has experienced one of the fastest declines in population growth ever seen in the world, second only to China, and in Brazil, in sharp contrast with China, the decline has been implemented without the support of the authorities.'

The annual population growth rate in Brazil fell from 2.9 per cent in the 1960s to 1.9 per cent in the 1980s (Table 3); today it is estimated at 1.6 per cent. The decline in fertility has occurred in all regions of the country, except the north, which is still receiving hundreds of thousands of migrants from the rest of the country.

Table 3 Average Annual Population Growth

	1960/70	1970/80	1980/91
North	3.5	5	5.2
North-east	2.4	2.2	1.8
South-east	2.7	2.6	1.8
South	3.5	1.4	1.4
Centre-west	5.6	4.1	2
Brazil	2.9	2.5	1.9

Source: IBGE Censuses, various years

The decline in fertility is extraordinary; in 1980 a woman had on average 4.3 children – by 1991 she was having just 2.7 children. The decline has largely been achieved by the use of the pill, available over the counter in chemists, and sterilisation, which is still not technically permitted in state hospitals but is carried out semi-illegally. According to Elza Berquió, one of the country's leading demographers:

Most Brazilian women today are determined to limit the size of their families. Brazil has no system of social welfare. Seeing children begging and stealing on the streets every day is a constant reminder to women of what can happen to their children if they can't provide for them. Sterilisation has become the easiest and most effective option.

As a result, nine million out of the 49 million Brazilian women of child-bearing age (14-49) have been sterilised.

Though avidly demanded by many Brazilian women, sterilisation may not always be the best solution, according to Elza Berquió:

I've nothing against sterilisation. In fact, it is being used by more and more women in industrialised countries. The only problem is that it is not always the right method. A young woman with one or two children may want to stop having children for a while, but to keep the option of having more children later. It is this kind of woman who is being sterilised in Brazil, when really it is not appropriate for her.

Another indication of the reluctance of women to have unwanted children is the high level of abortions, estimated at 1.4 million a year. Because it is actually a criminal offence to have an abortion, except in very restricted circumstances, women resort to expensive private clinics or, if they cannot afford this, to dangerous back-street practitioners. In a courageous decision, the first PT mayor of São Paulo, Luiza Erundina, created the first public abortion clinic in Brazil. It was a highly controversial decision of questionable legality.

The demographic revolution seems to have helped mitigate the severity of the social crisis. Though income has undoubtedly become more concentrated over recent decades, some important social indicators have improved. The per capita daily intake of calories has gradually increased, from an average of 2,320 in 1961-62, to 2,690 in 1988-90. Infant mortality rates have fallen to a 1990 estimate of 45 per 1,000 live births. Life expectancy is still low, particularly if compared with countries with lower per capita incomes – Chile, 72 years (with per capita GDP of US$2,160), Argentina, 71 years (US$2,790) and Brazil, 66 years (US$2,940) – but it is increasing, particularly in the north-east (64 years in 1980, compared with 54 years in 1970). The rate of serious malnutrition has dropped, from 17.8 per cent of the population in 1975 to 11.7 per cent in 1989.

* * *

Far from passively accepting their lot, the excluded millions are doing everything they can to force their way into the modern world. In the early morning in any shanty town in São Paulo, hundreds of young men and women set off for work. They may well be earning only the minimum wage as a maid or office boy or even be picking up odd jobs in the street, but many will be wearing fashionable clothes – mini-skirts, tight Lycra blouses, jeans and trainers. They will not have paid the full retail price for these goods; maids beg for skirts and blouses from the middle-class women they work for, boys buy trainers smuggled in from Paraguay, girls working as shop assistants get a discount on stock that has not sold well. Despite their poverty, these youngsters are trying desperately to be part of the modern world, mimicking the life style they see in TV soap operas every evening.

The 'excluded' have taken a series of measures to mitigate the impact of the social crisis. By having fewer children, women can allocate more scarce resources to each child. Brazil's huge informal market of street vendors and self-employed artisans, believed to be almost as big as the formal economy, may be allowing more resources to trickle down to the poor than is suggested by official figures. Above all, the extraordinarily strong feelings of solidarity that exist in Brazil's extended family networks, particularly among migrants from the north-east, help to save the poor from starvation. Maybe only one person in a shanty-town shack has a proper job, but his or her income will be helping feed ten or eleven people.

However, these personal survival mechanisms are both limited in their effectiveness and inadequate as a national response. The great challenge facing the PT is to channel the enormous vitality of Brazilian society into an organised and coherent programme, capable of producing a viable alternative to neoliberalism. Much is already being achieved, through the powerful alliance of the PT and huge mass-based organisations, particularly the powerful union federation, the CUT, which together are raising public awareness. More and more Brazilians seem ashamed at the way their society is dealing with the very poor and the marginalised, and believe that it is wrong for the president of a bank to earn a hundred times more than the woman who cleans his office. In 1992 the social scientist Herbert de Souza, universally known as Betinho, adopted a proposal first made by Lula and launched an emergency campaign to tackle hunger. Frail and infected by HIV through a contaminated blood transfusion, Betinho received an extraordinary response to his appeal. Thousands of local groups sprang up, opening soup kitchens, distributing food parcels and collecting old clothes, food and money.

More recently, Betinho has changed the focus of his campaign to concentrate primarily on job creation, which, he says, is the only lasting solution. He is well aware of the difficulties he faces:

We must confront the challenge of generating jobs in a society – modern society – that is based upon unemployment. Today a businessman says with pride, 'I am going to invest so many million dollars in a factory that will manufacture such-and-such a product, and it is so modern, so automated, that it will have virtually nobody working in it.' Now when 'modern' becomes synonymous with 'unemployment' we have to stop and think. When 'modern' means excluding people from social processes that they were previously part of, through their labour; when modern means creating a world of infinite production and impossible consumption, because people no longer have a job or an income, then we are heading for a kind of schizophrenia that is socially extremely dangerous.

Betinho's campaign has highlighted the key challenge facing the PT: coming up with a viable proposal for bringing real development – food, education, health care, environmental awareness – to the millions of excluded Brazilians, in a world in which economic success seems only to be achievable by neoliberal, market-oriented societies prepared to go to any lengths to reduce costs and compete successfully on the world market.

Profile: Benedita da Silva

52-year old Benedita, Brazil's first black senator, remembers as a child delivering laundry to the house of President Juscelino Kubitschek in Leme in Rio de Janeiro. Her mother, a washer-woman, was a *mae-de-santo*, a priestess in the Afro-Brazilian candomblé religion. 'At that time, it wasn't respectable for public figures to be seen consulting a *mae-de-santo*', recalls Benedita, 'so they came secretly at night.' Benedita, one of 13 children, spent her childhood in a shanty town built on stilts in a flooded area of Rio de Janeiro. The family was poor and from the age of six Benedita worked, first in street markets and then as a maid. 'Then I got a job in a smart nursery. I cleaned the bottoms of several leading public figures, whom I now meet as an equal', she laughs.

Benedita married at 15, just after her mother's death. By the time she was 22, she had five children. Her first husband, a house painter, was a heavy drinker. Even so, she stayed with him until his death 22 years later. Life was hard. In 1968 she could no longer earn enough to support herself and her children. 'I belong to the poorest of the poor in Brazilian society', she says. 'I'm one of the da Silvas of this life.' [In Brazil, da Silva is the commonest working-class surname] She felt suicidal until a friend took her to one of the evangelical churches, the Assembly of God. It got her over this difficult period and she has been a devoted follower ever since, even giving up Carnival which she used to enjoy enormously.

'After the bible, the PT' says Benedita. She was a founder member of the party and has been enormously active. Throughout her political career, she has turned the triple discrimination that she suffers into an electoral asset, using as her slogan, 'I am black, a woman and a shanty-town dweller.' She was a municipal councillor, then a federal deputy, becoming particularly active in the Constituent Assembly, which in 1987 drew up Brazil's new constitution. She presented 92 amendments, 25 of which were approved, including the controversial measure to make the job of maid a proper, regulated profession.

Benedita is a vehement defender of Brazil's black population, 'The Brazilian nation was forged through the rape of the black population', she says. 'Black families were destroyed. My grandparents and great-grandparents were slaves. They had children who were taken away from them and sold. We have no idea what happened to them.' Even today, Benedita suffers from discrimination. 'I go to the front entrance of apartment blocks and the porters still tell me to go round to the tradesmen's entrance.'

Benedita married for a second time in 1982. Her husband was a north-easterner with a long history of political involvement. In their heated political discussions, he cited Marx and Benedita replied with quotations from the Bible. He died in 1988 and Benedita married again, this time to the famous actor, Antônio Pitanga. Benedita waxes lyrical, 'I love my husband. I'm over the moon, passion 24 hours a day.'

Benedita has come up in the world. She is travelling widely and loves it. During a recent trip to Paris, she went to an official reception and was introduced to President François Mitterand. 'I spent so many years of my life working as a maid for rich madames in Brazil that I know how to sit at a banquet table and how to use the cutlery,' she jokes.

Benedita still lives in the Chapeu Mangueira shanty town, where she brought up her children. Like most shanty towns in Rio, it is located on a hillside, forcing visitors to climb up 56 steep steps to get to Benedita's house. Though her three-roomed house is much more comfortable than most of the others, she still suffers from periodic police 'invasions', water shortages and electricity blackouts. A few years ago one of her nephews was killed in a shoot-out. Benedita justifies her decision to stay in the shanty town by saying, *Sou favelada, estou senadora*, using the two verbs in Portuguese for 'to be', to say that her condition of life is to be a shanty-town dweller, whereas she is only temporarily a senator.

3

Lula: The Making of a Leader

When it was founded in 1980, the freshness of the PT's vision won the support of thousands of young industrial workers who had been brought up under the military dictatorship, when left-wing parties were banned. Bombarded by pro-government propaganda on the television and radio, the vast majority of these workers did not define themselves as left-wing, let alone socialist; most of them probably adhered to the practice, widespread at the time, of using the word *comunista* as a routine swearword. But they knew what they wanted: better wages, better working conditions, greater political freedom, and the right to reorganise their trade union movement so that it would truly represent their interests.

Luís Inácio da Silva quickly emerged as the leader of this new labour movement. Lula is a born leader with a remarkable capacity to captivate an audience. Factory workers will happily stand for half an hour or more, in the hot sun or pouring rain, listening to him. He thinks well on his feet and speaks from the heart, as he explained in a recent interview:

> I don't know if it is a weakness or not, but, to speak frankly, I often prefer to rely on my intuition than to work things out in my head. I think that intuition lets you put a bit of your heart in things, and I think to do politics without your heart makes people very hard, very realistic. And I don't think that that's good in politics. I don't think that you can be a good politician without deep human feelings, and I don't want to lose that side of me.

Brazil's industrial workers feel an immediate affinity with Lula who, until he became a national figure, had lived a life much like their own. He was born on 27 October 1945 in Garanhuns in the poor north-eastern state of Pernambuco. His parents were impoverished subsistence peasants and Lula was the seventh of eight children. Shortly after he was born, his father, like hundreds of thousands of others from the north-east, made the long journey down to the state of São Paulo, in search of work. He got a job in the docks in the port of Santos, loading bags of coffee. The first time Lula remembers seeing his father was when he came back to visit the family, when Lula was five years old.

Back in Pernambuco, Lula's mother, Eurídice Ferreira de Mello, struggled to feed and educate her children. Often they went to bed hungry. Overwhelmed by the effort, Lula's mother decided in December 1952 to leave the north-east and, with her eight children, to join her husband in São Paulo state. The 3,000km journey, in the back of an open lorry, took them 13 days. At first, the family went to live with the father in Vicente de Carvalho, a poor neighbourhood in the seaside resort of Guarujá, near Santos. To boost the family income, Lula, aged seven, sold peanuts, tapioca and oranges in the streets.

But the reunion between Lula's parents did not work out. Like so many other Brazilian men, Lula's father had started living with another woman – in fact, a cousin to his first wife – during the years he was separated from his first family. In 1956 Eurídice decided to move with her children to São Paulo. Partly perhaps because he never knew his father properly, Lula developed a very close and warm relationship with his mother. Even today he refers frequently to his mother's pride and happiness when he finally got his technical diploma and his regret that she did not live long enough to see him running for the presidency. It is an experience with which many poor Brazilian men and women can identify, in a country with a high level of internal migration and, as a result, numerous broken marriages.

Once in São Paulo, the whole family lived in a single room behind a bar. They had to share the toilet with the customers. Later Lula recalled his embarrassment at inviting friends home from school because there was no chair for them to sit on. It was then, he says, that for the first time he realised that his family was poor. At 12, Lula got his first full-time job, working in a dry cleaners. After being sacked, he looked around for other odd jobs, working as a boot-black and then as an office-boy. He got these jobs in the informal labour market, with none of the benefits guaranteed in the labour legislation.

At 14, Lula got his first registered job, working in a warehouse. Later he found work in an engineering company and, as a result, managed to enrol on a three-year part-time course to train as a lathe operator. During this period he had an accident during a night shift. He was replacing a nut on a machine while a colleague held down the brake, but his colleague nodded off. The blade slipped forward, cutting off Lula's little finger on his left hand; he was 18 years old at the time. Apart from work, his main interests were girls and football. He was a keen supporter of the Corinthians football club in São Paulo.

In 1966 Lula started work at Villares, one of the biggest engineering firms in the country. In May 1969 he married Maria de Lourdes, a young worker in a textile factory. The following year both Maria and her baby died during labour. She had been suffering from hepatitis, but it had not been diagnosed by the doctors. In 1973 Lula had a brief relationship with a young nurse, Miriam Cordeiro. In a development that was to have important political consequences later, they had a daughter and called her Luriam, following the practice common among the Brazilian working class of inventing a new name by combining the father's name with the mother's. The following year Lula married Marisa Letícia, a widow with one son. Marisa and Lula have three children, all boys.

So far, there had been nothing to distinguish Lula's life from that of thousands of other migrants from the north-east with similar tales of hunger, suffering and limited social advancement, despite years of effort. But Lula then shot to national prominence as the leader of the massive waves of strikes that swept through São Paulo's industries in 1978 and 1979 and by setting up what has become Latin America's most important left-wing political party. In telling the story, we shall as far as possible use Lula's own words and those of his colleagues, using testimony recorded by several authors, particularly the Chilean sociologist, Marta Harnecker, in her excellent book, *O Sonho era Possível*. Other sources include *Without Fear of Being Happy*, by Emir Sader and Ken Silverstein and *Lula, O Metalúrgico: Anatomia de uma Liderança*, by Marco Morel.

* * *

According to Lula, his first contact with the union movement came through his brother, José Ferreira da Silva, known as Friar Chico because of his monk-like hair cut. As a member of the banned Brazilian Communist Party, Lula's brother was active in underground politics. In 1969 he asked Lula, then working at an engineering plant in São Bernardo, an industrial town on the outskirts of São Paulo, to stand on his slate in the elections for the directorate of the metalworkers' union of São Bernardo and Diadema. Lula recalls:

> I was a lathe operator, I was earning reasonably well and I had a girlfriend. I wanted to play football, I wanted to go out dancing, I didn't want to know about union matters.

After reluctantly agreeing to stand and being elected, Lula gradually became more involved in the union, but never followed his brother into the Communist Party. Though he refused to define himself ideologically, he became firmly opposed to the existing union leadership.

In 1975 he was elected union president, with 92 per cent of the vote. At that time the union federation was controlled by *pelegos*, conservative union leaders who worked closely with the employers. Oddly enough, Lula was nominated for the presidency by the outgoing union head, Paulo Vidal, one of the old guard. With hindsight, Lula believes he was being used in an internal power struggle:

> I had never spoken at a union assembly, had never used a microphone, so – and this is a supposition – when Paulo agreed to nominate me he was planning to prove – not just to the directorate, but to all the workers as well – that he was irreplaceable and that I was a shit and couldn't get a damn thing done.

If this was Paulo Vidal's hidden agenda, his plan back-fired. A turning point for Lula came the year he was elected. His brother, Friar Chico, was arrested and charged with being a Communist 'subversive'. Lula learnt of his brother's arrest during a brief stopover in the United States on his way back from a conference in Japan, his first trip abroad. When a lawyer advised Lula to stay in the USA for a while, until the situation cooled down, Lula is reported to have replied:

> Look my friend, I don't speak the language of the people here, I've got no money, the food stinks, there's no rice, no beans. I'd rather be arrested in Brazil than stay in this dump of a country.

According to Lula, the arrest was:

> the main reason why I lost all my inhibitions. Before, I had been a typical union leader. I had been afraid of being arrested. I had been worried about my family. I had never thought that being a union activist required very much. But, after my brother was arrested, I lost my fear.

But, as we shall see, his recollection contradicts the testimony of several other activists, particularly that of the actress, Lélia Abramo. Lula may have lost his inhibitions, but not, it seems, his fear.

Buoyed up by his new militancy, Lula sought to change the way unions operated, improvising as he went along. When he took over, unions were largely apolitical. Workers did not look to them to support demands for higher wages or better working conditions. Members mostly went to the unions to obtain subsidised health treatment and other social benefits. They only sprang into life during the annual wage negotiations, and even then the wage increase was often worked out behind closed doors. In keeping with the government's wage policy at the time, there was no direct bargaining between unions and employers; wage increases were set by the government for the whole industry. Lula and the other young union leaders working with him decided that all this must change, but they began by making what seemed to be small changes:

Our first big decision was not just to wait for workers to come to union assemblies at the time of our annual wage increase, but for us to seek them out at the factory gates and get them involved in other issues. We knew we had to get the workers to have more trust in us. So do you know what I did? I started to arrange football championships: the union leadership against factory teams. Before the matches began, I used to talk to the workers for five minutes. After the game we had a few beers and cooked a barbecue.

The union leaders also tried to make the issues more accessible. Lula again:

I noticed that workers used to throw away the bulletin we gave them at the factory gates, when they were 50 yards or so down the road. I realised that they were chucking it away because it had nothing in it that interested them. So we decided to liven it up, to introduce cartoons, to turn it into an attractive four-page leaflet. The result: the workers didn't throw it away but put it in their pocket to read inside the factory.

In a short time, we managed to create a new awareness. Before, the union building had always been empty, no one took part in anything, but soon all our assemblies were crowded. What was the great advantage in doing this? It was to make the worker feel that the union belonged to him, was a body that would fight for him, go on the offensive for him. For instance, we did something that the workers loved – we printed in our journal the names of the line managers who treated them unfairly. In all, I think we achieved in three years things that normally in this country would have taken thirty.

From the beginning Lula insisted on his own approach. Another union leader, Paulo Skromov, recalls:

Lula had an interesting, if disconcerting, way of doing things. For example, when he was re-elected president of the union, I think it was in January 1978 – he was still very thin, and wore flares – he invited the São Paulo state governor and the Commander of the Second Army to the ceremony. For us, trade unionists on the left, this was completely nuts, this idea of inviting such authorities. He managed to upset both the right and the left.

In this unconventional way, Lula and the other leaders developed a union movement that in 1978 was able to mount the first serious challenge to the military government. Rejecting the wage rise offered by the government, the metalworkers opted for industrial action. The strike erupted in the Saab-Scania truck company in São Bernardo, spreading rapidly to other multinational companies such as Ford, Mercedes-Benz, Volkswagen and Chrysler. By the end of the second week, about 80,000 workers were on strike. Lula:

It was the first general strike since 1968 and it received enormous support from all over the country. In its way our 1978 strike meant for Brazilians what the Gdansk strike meant for the Poles. It was the first time that the Brazilian working class had shown such strength.

Far more than the other strike leaders, Lula was determined not to allow left-wing intellectuals to rush in and take over control of the strike movement. He stopped students from joining the pickets outside the factory gates, saying that they shouldn't get directly involved in a workers' struggle. To the irritation of some of his supporters, he frequently repeated a phrase made famous by a samba school in Rio, 'It's intellectuals who love poverty. What the poor like is luxury.'

One of the big names in Brazilian theatre, a committed left-wing actress called Lélia Abramo, recalls:

I wanted to get involved in the strike movement so I went to São Bernardo to see Lula, but he refused to talk to me. He had something against artists, students and intellectuals. But the others – Djalma Bom, Devanir and Jacó Bittar – they didn't feel the same way. In the end, I managed to be quite useful. As I had been in Europe during the war, I knew how to distribute food parcels. I showed Devanir how to weigh out the rice in 1kg, 2kg bags and so on. He was very grateful. And in this way I got to know Lula. He finally started to talk to me and we became close friends.

The 1978 strike took the government and the manufacturers completely by surprise. By the end of May, the union had won a 24.5 per cent pay rise from the manufacturers, much more than their original offer. But according to Lula, the wage increase was not the strike's main achievement:

The great victory, even more than the wage rise, was that we forced the companies to negotiate an agreement directly with the union, without government interference.

Other strikes soon erupted in a number of industries around the country. By the end of the year, over half a million workers were on strike and many won pay rises above those authorised by the government. The government's wage policy had come under serious threat for the first time.

By the following year, however, the government was better prepared. The metalworkers' union in São Bernardo called a general strike for 13 March, demanding a pay increase and improved working conditions. The response was overwhelming. The general assemblies, called by the union, had to be held in the Vila Euclides football stadium, the only place capable of holding more than 80,000 people. Lula describes the first assembly:

When we [the union leaders] arrived, the fences, the stadium, the grass, everywhere was full of people, and the podium was only a little table. The sound system wasn't even big enough for a small room, and I was alone, like a clown, on top of the table. Everyone was getting tense, and the leaders were beginning to argue, because the sound system wasn't any good and who knows what else was wrong... And the workers said, 'Calm down, calm down'. You know what we did? We kept them there for four hours on the field without sound... I yelled, the people in front of me repeated what I'd said and it was passed backwards ... When it started to rain, a few people started to leave. I shouted that no one there would dissolve in the rain and nobody else went away.

The strike was soon declared illegal, but Lula, showing a new willingness to take on the authorities, told a union assembly, 'They can declare the strike illegal, but it is just and legitimate, because its illegality is based on laws that weren't made by us and our representatives'. The experience was important for all the new union leaders, as Lula recalls:

I think that the first big lesson for us was that not one of us, individually, believed that we could do what we did. None of us believed that every blessed day, come sun come rain, we could get 90,000 workers in a football stadium. And when we were gathered there, all together, we realised that if we pooled our courage, together we became a giant. Individually, we all had qualms. We thought, 'we can't do this, we can't do that'. But together we did things that individually we thought impossible.

The union leaders were exhilarated by the political forces they had awakened. Paulo Skromov:

It's something that happens rarely in history – that a mass-based movement erupts on the world stage at precisely the right moment, when there are sensitive leaders to take charge of it. At that time we weren't deluding ourselves when we said that we were going to transform the country, that we were creating a force that could free us from exploitation, from oppression. We were doing something of extreme importance. We were making history. There is nothing more exciting, more stimulating for mankind than to dream, and to believe that you can transform that dream into reality.

It was during the strike that Lula discovered his formidable talent for public speaking. Lula, who had never been very keen on reading books, had his own way of preparing his speeches, according to Paulo Skromov:

Lula is someone who knows how to listen. He used to extract the best things from what he heard and make notes on his hand. He prepared his speeches with five, six or seven notes scribbled on the back of his hand... Lula's speeches captivated people. They were rich in content and extraordinarily rich in form. People listened to him for half an hour and thought he had been speaking for two minutes at most. They wanted more. I remember very well how people looked when they were listening to him. They looked as if they were drinking and were savouring every drop.

But there were also difficult moments, says Lula, 'During the 1979 strike, our union was taken over by the police for 15 days. It was the first confrontation we had ever had with armed police, police dogs, firemen.'

According to Lula, there was also a time when he disappeared from view, because the union's executive committee feared his arrest and ordered him to lay low. But the full story seems to have been more complicated. The human rights lawyer, Luis Eduardo Greenhalgh, who was deeply involved in the new union movement from the early days, recalls:

The Commander of the Second Army phoned Lula and threatened him, 'You go to the assemblies and you'll be arrested'. Lula, who had never had any contact with the army's brutal counter-insurgency units, ended up staying away from the assemblies.

The other union leaders tried to make up for Lula's absence, remembers Paulo Skromov:

Djalma Bom – he was the number two in the union – tried to take over Lula's role. But he didn't have the same impact as Lula, he didn't have his charisma. Though the workers trusted all the leaders, they wanted Lula. He had this incredible gift, something very personal. After two days like this, holding assemblies that attracted fewer and fewer people, we realised that the strike was losing momentum.

Several of the union leaders, together with Lélia Abramo, found out where Lula was hiding and went there. Paulo Skromov:

We went into the house and found him, dressed in shorts, playing with his children on the carpet in the living room.

Lélia Abramo takes up the story:

41

David de Moraes said, 'We've come here to find out what's happened. It would be a good idea for you to go to the next assembly.' David's understated words would have been enough to persuade most people, but Lula didn't react. He stayed sitting on the floor, without saying anything. Then I asked if any other union leader wanted to speak. No one did. I'm telling you this not to talk about myself, but to tell you how it happened. So I said: 'Look, Lula, I didn't come here to praise you or to complain about you. I came her to tell you that you are coming with me to the assembly. I'm going to take you there.'

According to Paulo Skromov:

Lélia was wonderful, incredible. We didn't know what to say to Lula, but he listened to her and then turned to us and said, 'You're right. I reckon I'm wrong. I'll come back with you.'

Lula adds:

I had been banned by the authorities. It wasn't easy to take over running the strike again. But when I realised that what I was doing was causing serious problems for the movement, I decided to go back, even if it meant putting my neck on the guillotine.

Lélia Abramo continues:

I took him back. We went into the large room. It was packed. There must have been about 2,000 people there. He walked around the room and then, when he reached the head table, he burst into tears, started to sob. He was cheered. It lasted for at least ten minutes. He recovered himself and made a wonderful speech. For the first time he aligned himself politically with the opposition. He had never done this before.

Even so, the strike was by no means an unqualified success. On 21 March, eight days after the strike began, the labour minister agreed to talks between the unions and their employers, but insisted first on an immediate return to work by the strikers. This was overwhelmingly rejected by the strikers, but after heavy intimidation by the military police, many people began to drift back to work. In an effort to limit the damage, Lula accepted the employers' proposal for a 45-day truce and a 15 per cent wage rise, in exchange for a promise not to carry out reprisal sackings of union militants.

Lula's handling of the negotiations was bitterly criticised by many workers and some of his fellow union leaders. He was even jeered in the stadium when he explained his actions, according to Paulo Skromov:

We thought he had made a terrible mistake. Jacó began to cry. I tried to comfort him, but I was feeling much the same myself.

Lula:

Many workers left the stadium that night calling me a traitor, saying that I had sold them down the river, that I had betrayed them. It was a very difficult period for me. Political scientists said that I would never again be able to organise a strike, to regain the confidence of the workers. Paulo Skromov said that I was politically destroyed.

Paulo Skromov:

I was having lunch with Lula shortly afterwards, in the union canteen. A worker came up to our table and angrily threw down his union membership card in front of Lula. We looked at Lula. It was fairly tense. But Lula only lowered his head and the worker eventually walked off. Lula turned to us and said, 'That's nothing compared to what I've had to go through since the end of the strike.'

But some union leaders supported Lula. Wagner Benevides:

Many workers thought that we could have continued, but it wasn't true. The strike had to stop. Everyone was exhausted. It had reached a critical moment. We had to opt... And Lula recovered. He was born again out of the ashes.

The 1979 strike convinced Lula and other union leaders of the need to create their own political party. They had received minimal support from Congress, even from those who claimed to be part of the opposition, which strengthened their distrust of professional politicians. The engineering companies subsequently reneged on their promise not to carry out reprisal sackings, further convincing the union leaders that they needed to take part directly in politics to fight for fairer laws on industrial action. A new phase in Brazilian history was about to begin.

Profile: Olívio Dutra

Olívio, who comes from the progressive wing of the Catholic Church, is one of the PT's founder members. He was born in the small town of São Luis Gonzaga in the southerly state of Rio Grande do Sul. His mother was a commited Catholic, recalls Olívio, 'She liked to take us to mass, but only if we had decent clothes to wear. If we didn't, which was often, as we were poor, she used to make us pray at home.' His father, a carpenter, was not a practising Catholic but was determined to see his children educated. As he worked for the local priests, he got them to persuade the Catholic college to accept Olívio.

In 1961, Olívio went to work in a bank. He was soon involved in organising a strike and was promptly transferred by the bank from São Luis Gonzaga to the state capital, Porto Alegre. 'They sent me to the poorest agency, on the outskirts of the city, no doubt hoping to isolate me,' says Olívio. But it didn't work out like that. Partly because Olívio was very active in the grassroots work of the progressive wing of the Catholic Church, he became increasingly politicised. 'I was a Marxist Christian,' says Olívio, 'Christian above all, with my Marxism developing, stage by stage.'

In 1975, Olívio was elected president of the Porto Alegre bank clerks' union. Just like Lula in São Bernardo and Diadema, Olívio revolutionised the way the union worked. 'I was determined to get the union out to meet the base, to make contact with ordinary bank clerks,' he remembers. 'We also created new links with other unions, making contact with the health union, because the main hospital was just nearby, and with the metalworkers.' Increasing the militancy of the bank clerks was uphill work. 'All this was happening under military rule, with all that propaganda about the "Brazilian miracle". Many people were enthusiastic about the way the military were modernising the ports, the communications system, the financial system.'

Olívio helped found the PT in Rio Grande do Sul and, in one of the national party's most significant victories, was elected mayor of Porto Alegre in 1988. During his four-year term of office, he placed great stress on increasing popular participation in local government (see page 87). He finished with 55 per cent of the population expressing approval for what he had done. The vice-mayor, Tarso Genro won a comfortable victory in 1992.

In October 1994, Olívio ran for the state governorship of Rio Grande do Sul against strong competition from the former Social Minister, Antonio Brito. With the backing of the powerful PMDB party machine, Brito was expected to win a comfortable victory in the first round, but Olívio made a late comeback. The news magazine, *Veja*, commented, 'Olívio Dutra pulled off a real feat. He managed to win votes by criticising the *Real* (new currency), repeating endlessly on television that the economic plan had been launched just to get Fernando Henrique elected.' Olívio got through to the second round, but was beaten by Brito in a close contest in November.

4
Building the Party

In the shape of Lula, the stubborn, non-intellectual leader, the Brazilian Left rediscovered the myth of the revolutionary worker. Various Trotskyist groups, veterans of Brazil's Socialist Party and former urban guerrillas were immediately attracted to the new party. Most of the people who had lost relatives during the military dictatorship also joined up. It was the moment for all 'anti-Stalinists' to get together. The PT even gave an unexpected lease of life to old-time socialists who had nearly lost all hope, winning enthusiastic support from such veterans as Clara Scharf, wife of the famous urban guerrilla leader, Carlos Marighella; Apolônio de Carvalho, one of Brazil's volunteers in the International Brigades of the Spanish Civil War and Mário Pedrosa, the country's leading arts critic and a widely respected Trotskyist.

Support for the PT was not, however, universal on the left. Its creation came as a serious blow both to the two Communist parties in Brazil – the Soviet-aligned Brazilian Communist Party (PCB) and the Chinese-aligned Communist Party of Brazil (PC do B) – and to MR-8, a split from the PCB that had aligned itself with the *pelego* union officials. The PT challenged all these parties' claims to be the 'vanguard of the working class' and some intellectuals, reluctant to relinquish ideas that they had held for years, fought back.

The new party provoked important theoretical debates on the left, challenging indirectly the idea of compromise so widely accepted in Brazilian society. Until then, few political activists had defied the Communist Party's *diktat* that all 'progressive' forces should work together. This doctrine was justified by the theory that Brazil was a dual society, ruled by a backward rural oligarchy in alliance with imperialism, that was being challenged by a new class of national industrialists.

The solution, it was argued, was to align with the industrialists in order to modernise Brazil. It was a dualist logic that took many forms: modernity versus backwardness; national bourgeoisie versus imperialism; capitalism versus feudalism. Before the emergence of the PT, the dogma had already come under attack at a theoretical level. In 1962 an influential social scientist, Francisco de Oliveira, had written an essay called 'The critique of dualist reason', which had become the bible for all those exasperated

46

with the dualist approach. He had argued that backwardness was not in conflict with capitalism, but a necessary condition of it. If accepted, his argument destroyed the Communist Party's theoretical justification for the alliances it forged with modern capitalist groups. In founding the PT, a party created by and for the very class that the Communists claimed to be defending, Lula had provided a practical alternative to the Communist Party's multi-class strategy.

As intellectuals and exiled political leaders began to discuss Lula's idea of a Workers' Party, a split immediately appeared. Most intellectuals, including Almino Afonso, labour minister in the government of President João Goulart, overthrown by the military in 1964, and Francisco Weffort, a political scientist who had written a highly influential essay on the collapse of populism, agreed that the 1978 and 1979 strikes had created a new working class leadership and had been decisive in weakening the regime. But most objected to the creation of a class-oriented party, wanting instead a democratic socialist party. In particular, the influential sociologist, Fernando Henrique Cardoso, a former Communist who had been forced into exile in the 1960s, strongly objected to the idea of such a party, claiming that this was tantamount to reducing social relations to labour relations. He also argued that the 'new unionists' were falling into the trap set by the military government's new electoral law, which hoped to divide the opposition by encouraging a plethora of new parties. Cardoso doubted whether a party led by workers would obtain the support of ten per cent of Congress, which was one of the conditions in the electoral law for the registration of new political parties.

Lula and the union leaders were undeterred. While welcoming into the party members of the opposition in Congress, they reiterated that the new party would represent workers directly and not be represented by others.

Fernando Henrique Cardoso and Almino Afonso withdrew from the project, joining the only left-of-centre party permitted during the worst years of military rule, the MDB, later to be rechristened the Party of the Brazilian Democratic Movement (PMDB). Many intellectuals shared Fernando Henrique Cardoso's view that workers by themselves did not have the knowledge needed to run a party, far less govern the country. In this sense, they shared the views of classical Marxists such as Kautsky and Lenin, for whom political consciousness had to be brought to workers from outside their working world.

Others, however, disagreed. Many intellectuals, particularly those who had studied the Brazilian working class, rethought their position and joined the party. Among them were the political scientist Francisco Weffort, the economist Paul Singer, and the historian Marco Aurélio Garcia, and the philosopher Marilena Chauí. It was an impressive group. Some time later, after a crisis within the MDB narrowed the options for its left-wing, several other members of Congress joined the party. Among them were Irma

47

Passoni, a Catholic activist and one of the founder members of the Cost of Living Movement, which had got thousands into the streets in the 1970s in protest over the military's economic policy, the human rights lawyer, Ayrton Soares, who had defended political prisoners, and the economist, Eduardo Suplicy.

* * *

The 1978 and 1979 strikes increased the confidence of union leaders and strengthened Lula's position, giving impetus to the talks on setting up a new party. In August 1980, the PT was offically founded. Finally, workers had their own party, free from the control of government, clandestine political parties, intellectuals and even the unions themselves. The heavyweights of 'new unionism' were among the party's founders and all but four of the 16 members of the PT's first ruling body, the First National Provisional Commission, were union leaders. Over the following twelve months, excited by the new developments, members of thirty unions throughout the country voted *pelegos* out of office, replacing them with 'new unionists'.

The PT's first party manifesto suggests that, for all their bravado, the union leaders still had inner doubts over their capacity to become national political figures:

> We do not want to own the PT, all the more so because we sincerely believe that among the workers there are activists who are more prepared and more devoted than us; it will be for them to build and lead our party. We are only using our moral and political authority to create new space for the whole of the working class. The deep evils that affect Brazilian society will not be overcome without the decisive participation of the workers. The instrument for that is the PT.

It was also strongly workerist:

> A Workers' Party means a party without employers... We do not want to create just one more party... We want a party deeply committed to eliminate one man's exploitation by another... a party which contributes to the organisation and consciousness of the masses, the strengthening and ideological independence of the popular sectors, in particular workers...

The unionists wanted the PT not only to represent, at a political level, the interests of the workers, but also to be internally democratic and accountable to its members, both novel developments for a Brazilian political party. They opened their doors to a plethora of small left-wing groups, mass-based organisations and others, believing that, by joining the party, each

48

small group would make its own original contribution to the construction of the party. As Francisco Weffort realised at the time, this was part of the originality of the PT's experiment:

> What is the point of defining the party as a Marxist party? ... This goes against the uniqueness of our experiment ... We do need a better ideological definition but not a definition of the party in theoretical or philosophical terms ... What would we do with the non-Marxist socialists in the party, or the Catholics, if we redefined ourselves as a Marxist party? Would we expel them all?

The small groups wore their 'double shirts', as the double militancy was called, with openness and pride. To quote from the early document again:

> When asked whether wearing two shirts might not imply disloyalty to the party, our answer is straightforward; the revolutionary's shirt is the proletarian revolution and to wear it means helping to construct both the PT and a revolutionary organisation. They are complementary means of achieving the same aim, the overthrow of bourgeois power.

Nevertheless, all the small left-wing groups that joined the PT in 1980 did it with the aim of taking over the party leadership. Most wanted to transform it into a 'Marxist revolutionary' party, though they differed in the tactics they used and the theories they quoted. Many of these groups were influential, particularly in the terminology adopted by the party in the early years, but today it is clear that, after many internal struggles, the opposite has happened; rather than taking over the PT, most small groups have lost their identity, being absorbed into the PT during its process of dynamic growth. The party is still divided into several tendencies, but they are less well-organised and hermetic and no longer plot to conquer the party from within. They more closely resemble the different ideological factions found within any large heterogeneous party.

This process of absorption, however, was not easy. The struggle between the various tendencies hindered party growth in the areas where the small groups controlled the local party machinery. The weakest groups would usually make an alliance to defeat the strongest, in an ever-more debilitating process. It also brought to the party a scent of dogmatism and sectarianism that was not part of the union leaders' original pragmatic approach. Yet paradoxically, the need to tackle the problem of the party's 'double shirtists' helped to make the party more democratic. To ensure that no tendency gained control of the party, rules had to be drawn up for debating every proposal and for holding the debates according to strict rules. The party also had to be absolutely scrupulous in the way it held elections for delegates and party officers, including passing rules guaranteeing a minimum number of seats for under-represented groups such as blacks and women.

Some of the small groups used what were seen by the PT leadership as divisive tactics and in 1983 the original hard core of union leaders responded by creating their own tendency, called *Articulação 113*. As well as the main union leaders, its 113 members included most of the intellectuals in the party and the highly qualified cadres of the underground group, the National Liberation Action (ALN), which, under the leadership of Carlos Marighella, had launched Brazil's first urban guerrilla attacks in the late 1960s. The aim of this new tendency was to maintain the open character of the party and to keep it in close contact with mass-based movements. It was contradictory, in that the party's founding fathers were adopting the small groups' tactics to campaign against them, but it worked. *Articulação* won control of the party and was able to provide it with an identity and a unified command during periods of explosive growth.

Tolerance of factions began to be seriously questioned in 1985 when the communist parties were legalised and the military handed over power to a civilian adminstration. These parties could no longer appeal to the PT for protection from an authoritarian state, giving the green light to those who wanted to address openly the issue of double militancy. The issue came to a head in April 1986, after members of the tiny Brazilian Revolutionary Communist Party (PCBR), claiming to be *petistas*, were arrested while trying to rob a bank in the city of Salvador in the north-eastern state of Bahia. In a comment that became famous throughout the country, Lula said, 'I don't consider the attitude of those in Salvador to have been radical. It was imbecilic. There is a big difference between imbecility and radicalism.'

At a national meeting a month later, the PT's ruling body approved a resolution stating that tendencies would be permitted only if they accepted the party's programme and its internal discipline. Detailed rules were passed at later meetings, defining what constituted a tendency and denying recognition to factions that operated as independent parties. Slowly and painfully, the various small groups had to decide whether or not to conform to the new rules or leave the PT. They were given time to do so, but finally in 1993, not without pangs of guilt, the party expelled two Trotskyist groups that had refused to adhere to the new rules.

Articulação's control over the party came to an abrupt end in 1993. As Brazil's crisis deepened, the party moved to the left and, just before the 1993 National Congress, *Articulação* split into a centre group, made up mostly of union leaders and called 'Unity in struggle' (*Unidade na Luta*), and a 'Left option' (*Opção de Esquerda*), composed mainly of former ALN activists. No single group is today in control of the party, which is being run somewhat hesitantly by a coalition of all the factions. The new dominant groups are no more than unstable conglomerates of small groups, which change alliances according to the circumstances of the day. There is no clear stable majority and no leadership, apart from Lula. While linked to the centre group, Lula tries to stay above the disputes. Brought together by the apparent strength of Lula's chances in the presidential elections, the 1994 Congress marked a *rapprochement* between the various factions, particularly between the two tendencies in *Articulação*. This led to a temporary equilibrium, but with greater participation for the Left in the governing bodies.

* * *

Though the PT was set up by trade unionists, intellectuals have always played a central role in developing the party's political strategy. In the early days the key idea brought into the discussions by the intellectuals was the concept of hegemony, as developed by the Italian communist leader and theoretician, Antonio Gramsci. While Lenin had developed theories about the conditions for a victorious proletarian revolution during his years of exile in Siberia at the turn of the century, Gramsci spent eleven years in prison during the rule of Benito Mussolini, puzzling over why Italy's peasantry and petty bourgeoisie were supporting fascism. Gramsci's ideas seemed particularly appropriate to the founders of the PT, as they struggled to set up their party under the shadow of military rule.

Gramsci suggested that instead of seizing power through a decisive revolution led by a military-style party, as proposed by Lenin, positions should be gradually conquered on the political chessboard. Rather than crushing the business élite and alienating the middle classes, he proposed winning over the middle classes through persuasion. To do this he concluded that it was necessary to develop an alternative ideology that would supercede the dominant one, imposed by the ruling élite.

This Gramscian approach was reflected in resolutions passed during the first party Congress:

> The working class must develop a long-term policy of accumulating forces, which means disputing hegemony. Winning hegemony is a fundamental part of the strategy for the revolutionary transformation of Brazilian society.

According to the Gramscian concept of hegemony, it is necessary to build up gradually a dominant position within any given political situation. The PT has adopted this strategy at each stage of its development and in every sphere of activity. From the moment it is set up, every nucleus in the party attempts to build up its political presence, emphasising its differences with other political forces. It refuses to support more powerful political forces, going alone to the polls even when defeat is certain. Only when it becomes the dominant force does it propose alliances with other groups, under PT hegemony. This has been a recurrent pattern in the PT's development at national and local level. For example, when first targetting the trade unions, the PT in 1983 created, and exercised hegemony over, the central union body, the CUT. By 1988 the CUT had in turn achieved dominance over the wider union movement, becoming by far the most important workers' federation in Brazil.

The PT's drive for political hegemony was made easier by the rapid escalation of the Brazilian crisis. The only real obstacle was the equally spectacular growth of the Protestant evangelical churches, which took place at the same time. The evangelicals were seeking hegemony over people's souls and regarded the PT as their enemy, in a kind of combat between God and the Devil. While the PT's relations with the Catholic Church are a mix of closeness and rivalry, the party feels only antagonism towards the evangelical churches. The 1989 presidential campaign sparked off a virtual religious war between the Catholic Church, supporting Lula, and the evangelical denominations, supporting Collor.

For the 1989 presidential election, the PT created the Brazilian Popular Front through which it exerted clear hegemony over a wide spectrum of left-wing forces. Only the tiny former communist party, now called the Popular Socialist Party (PPS), had its own candidate. Although Lula was defeated, the PT emerged by the end of the campaign as the only mutually-acceptable representative of all left-wing forces, including those led by Leonel Brizola, the veteran populist leader, who almost defeated Lula in the first round but in the end had no alternative but to support him against the neoliberals represented by Fernando Collor de Mello.

For the 1994 campaign, a much more mature Lula tried to take the concept of political hegemony one step further. He decided to broaden the sphere of the PT's influence to include the whole of the middle class, small and medium-sized entrepreneurs, family farms and medium-sized landowners. He was helped in this endeavour by the collapse of the Berlin Wall and, with it, of any remaining belief in statism and class rule among the Brazilian Left. As part of his strategy, Lula wanted to win over to his alliance the faction within Fernando Henrique Cardoso's Social Democratic Party (PSDB) that was unhappy with that party's growing links with the Right. In early 1994, Lula met some of the main social democratic leaders, including the former state governors, Ciro Gomes and Tasso Jereissati. They agreed to work towards a joint programme. In exchange for the Social Democrats' support for Lula, the PT would back Mário Covas, their candidate for the governorship of São Paulo. Jereissati would also become the candidate for vice-president on Lula's ticket. It would have been a hugely important step in building the broad political front, under PT hegemony, long envisaged by Lula.

But his plans were thwarted by the accelerating Brazilian crisis, which radicalised the party. Leading PT cadres, particularly those linked to the

PT's candidate for the governorship of São Paulo, opposed the agreement, believing that the PT could win the presidency without further alliances.

The ideological conditions for this attempt could not have been more adverse. Neoliberalism was the dominant ideology; a forceful campaign was under way to privatise all state companies; civil servants were under attack for being highly-privileged and over-paid, and trade unions were being blamed for widespread unemployment. The foreign debt burden had eroded public finances to such an extent that education, health and social welfare services were collapsing and the state itself was being blamed. Throughout Latin America the neoliberal proposal for drastically reducing the state sector was being hailed by the mainstream press and by the ruling élite as the only solution to the region's economic crisis. Members of the middle class were seduced by the idea of private enterprise, of being able to set up their own family shop or small business.

Even though it had not actually solved Latin America's economic and social problems, neoliberalism had put progressive politicians on the defensive all over Latin America. It had become a culture, a set of values that preferred individualism to collectivism, competition over solidarity, USA fashions rather than popular culture. Just as young people in eastern Europe had hungered after western clothes prior to the fall of the Berlin Wall, Brazilians yearned for foreign products, made more accessible by Collor de Mello's reduction in tariff barriers.

Even at the time, some PT members were aware that this dominant ideology was creating serious problems for the party's strategy. 'The Left must have the humility to realise that it lacks a socialist project capable of winning over a broad majority, of achieving hegemony among them', warned Tarso Genro, the PT mayor of Porto Alegre, in an article published in the *Folha de S.Paulo*. Challenging the doctrinaire views expressed by many within the party, he proposed what he called 'a moratorium on Utopias', an ironic reference to the party's insistent demands for a moratorium on foreign debt repayments. Instead, Tarso Genro proposed the formation of a 'new historical bloc based on democracy and not any more on the idea of a "transition to socialism".' He added that 'scaling down our programme is the only way to confront the barbarity of social apartheid.'

Such views were ignored and the proposed alliance with the Social Democrats was rejected, even before proper discussions got under way. Instead of the PT winning over new supporters, a huge anti-Lula front emerged, involving the centre-left, the centre and the entire conservative camp. It was led by the then finance minister, Fernando Henrique Cardoso, the same renowned sociologist who, back in the late 1970s, after years of exile abroad, had been involved in the early discussions over the formation of the PT.

Profile: Flavio

A broad grin stretches across Flavio's face. 'My favourite things are ice cream, girls and politics,' he says. Fourteen-year-old Flavio is a PT *militante*. Although he will not be able to vote until he is 16, he proudly wears a 'Lula Brasil' T-shirt and makes the campaign's L for Lula sign with his hand. 'I like Lula's simplicity, modesty and humility,' he explains.

It was a different story in 1989. Aged nine, Flavio started supporting Lula but, influenced by the media campaign in favour of Fernando Collor de Mello, he changed his mind in mid-campaign. 'I asked my father if I could switch,' he explained. His family has always respected his ideas ever since he started reading political journals in his early childhood, so Flavio joined the local Collor support group. 'I thought that Collor would modernise Brazil, bring it out of the Third World.'

In 1992, Flavio, along with the rest of Brazil, discovered just how corrupt Collor was and transferred his allegiance back to Lula. 'Lula thinks about the poor. He should be our president. Fernando Henrique Cardoso may be honest, but he is linked to the old guard. They have been in power for too long and have done nothing to help Brazil.' But he doesn't rule out an alliance in the future with Cardoso. 'I wish there had been one back in 1993, because it would have made the PT stronger.'

Flavio believes that in politics you have to be driven just as much by your emotions as by your intellect. 'At a meeting I saw Lula pick up a street kid. He was crying. The whole experience moved me deeply.' Flavio gave his full backing to Lula's 1994 slogan, 'no child out of school'. 'When I see a child sleeping out rough under a flyover, I think that he or she needs a home, a mother, food and education,' he says. 'Education is a good place to start.'

Despite the recent decline in the birth rate, Brazil is still a country of young people. There are about sixty million youngsters under 17, about forty per cent of the population. At most PT rallies, it is the youth who make PT politics fun with the liberal use of face paint and colourful campaign costumes.

(Interview by Tony Samphier)

Profile: José Genoíno

Genoíno, 48 years old, is the PT leader that many *petistas* love to hate. Born into a poor rural family in the state of Ceará in the northeast, like millions of others, he migrated to the south of the country in search of work. He became active in left-wing politics in the 1960s and was forced underground by the military, joining an ill-fated attempt by left-wing activists to flee into the Amazon forest to prepare for a rural guerrilla war. The few dozen activists were soon discovered and were crushed in a major army offensive involving 15,000 troops.

Genoíno was one of the few to survive. Badly tortured, he was eventually convicted by a military court. After serving his sentence, he was released and immediately got involved in politics once again. In November 1982, he was elected federal deputy for the PT on the most radical of platforms. He has remained in Congress ever since, becoming one of the PT's most important leaders.

Genoíno now belongs to the moderate, parliamentary faction of the PT. In 1990 he and Tarso Genro, another original thinker, now mayor of Porto Alegre, wrote a series of articles, published in the *Folha de S.Paulo*, in which they called for far-reaching changes to the party's reform programme. One of the articles demanded an end to what it called 'left-wing radicalism', which, the authors claimed, was inflicting a great deal of damage on the whole socialist project. When criticised by some PT factions for betraying his earlier ideals, Genoíno replied, 'If I want to reform the world, I have to accept the challenge of being reformed myself.'

5
Running for Office

In 1982, just two years after its creation, the party decided to take part in elections, a decision that sparked controversy among party members. For the first time since the military coup in 1964, voters were able to choose state governors freely, as well as national, state and municipal representatives. These elections marked an important phase in the gradual process, strictly controlled by the military, of returning Brazil to civilian government. At this time most PT members, including Lula, thought that it would be extremely difficult, if not impossible, for the PT ever to be voted into power at a national level. According to its 1982 electoral charter, the main reason behind the party's decision to take part in elections was not to gain power but to use the experience 'as a tool in the organisation and mobilisation of workers and in building popular power'. How, eventually, this 'popular power' was to take over government was left vague, perhaps because many activists still did not trust the military's commitment to hand power to civilian politicians and so did not want to rule out entirely the option of insurrection.

The party established rigorous criteria for selecting candidates. They had to be approved by the nuclei; they had to have been active in workers' movements or in the party itself, and they had to agree, if elected, to donate forty per cent of their salary to party funds. In a deliberate attempt to break the elitist tradition of Brazilian politics, preference was given to working class candidates.

The PT put up candidates in most states in the country, but concentrated its efforts in São Paulo, the party's birthplace. Lula stood as the PT's candidate for the São Paulo state governorship, running with the slogan, 'A Brazilian like You', as part of the campaign against elitism. In São Paulo the PT attracted up to 100,000 people to its rallies, far more than any other party, but the election result fell well short of the expectations created by this success. Lula finished fourth, with just 10 per cent of the vote. Nationwide, the PT got 1.5 million votes, just 3.3 per cent of the total. This was less than the 5 per cent required for registration under the electoral law. The PT had elected just eight federal deputies (six of whom were from São Paulo), 12 state deputies, two mayors (including the mayor of Diadema, to be discussed in the next chapter) and 78 municipal councillors. Over seventy per cent of its total vote had been cast in São Paulo.

The results were disappointing. It seemed that the fundamental objective of many voters, including some PT supporters, was to defeat military-backed candidates, so they voted tactically, opting for the largest opposition party, the centrist PMDB, which gained control of 75 out of the 100 largest city councils in the country. In its first electoral foray, the PT was denied the protest vote it already believed belonged to it by right.

Lula recognised that he had made mistakes, saying later, 'Nobody wanted to be a Brazilian just like me. They wanted to be a Brazilian with better living conditions, with better trained minds, with a better quality of life.'

Many newspapers claimed that the PT had been dealt a death blow. A few months after the election, the conservative São Paulo newspaper, *O Estado de S.Paulo*, ran an exultant headline, 'After its First Test, the PT is Ending. Many Already Leaving the Party.' Though the party had suffered a setback, this article clearly contained a large dose of wishful thinking, exemplifying the biased reporting that has plagued the party since its foundation.

* * *

The PT soon bounced back. In 1983 the party began to mobilise the nation to demand direct elections for president in 1985, not the indirect election through an electoral college permitted by the military as part of its gradual process of political liberalisation. It was the kind of campaign with which PT activists felt completely at home, prompting none of the reservations that some still felt about taking part in elections. By late 1984 hundreds of thousands of demonstrators were taking part in massive rallies in many parts of the country as the campaign turned into a nationwide demand for an end to military rule. By then, other opposition parties were involved and, after weeks of unnatural silence, even Globo television was eventually forced to report the events.

The opposition alliance, however, failed by a handful of votes to obtain the two-thirds majority in Congress required to pass a constitutional amendment reinstating direct elections for president. All the opposition parties except the PT favoured the fall-back strategy, by which those in favour of direct elections challenged – and eventually beat – the government at its own game. After a series of behind-the-scenes negotiations, a majority in the electoral college was persuaded to vote for the opposition candidate, Tancredo Neves, a highly-respected elder statesman who had never allowed himself to be co-opted by the military, rather than for Paulo Maluf, the right-wing, authoritarian politician supported by the military.

In a highly controversial decision, reflecting the idealism of many PT activists, a majority of PT members decided, after a meticulously democratic consultation process, that its federal deputies should not take part in the vote in the electoral college. PT members felt that, after a hugely successful popular campaign in which real change had become possible, the Brazilian political élite had returned to its old practice of resolving everything behind closed doors. At the time, the PT's decision was widely criticised, even within the party. Critics argued that the PT's overriding objective ought to be to get the military out of power. Three federal deputies felt so strongly that they left the PT in order to vote in the electoral college. But the PT's decision was subsequently largely vindicated. As disillusion with the new civilian government grew, many Brazilians began to see the PT as the only political force that had had the courage to stick to its principles. What was just as important as getting rid of the military, many began to believe, was to create a new, authentically democratic political system to replace the military's authoritarian style of government.

In the short term, however, the PT's decision left it isolated and helped throw the party into one of its periodic crises. Gradually, the party recovered. It began to play down its insistence on being exclusively a party of workers, stressing instead its role as a mass-based party, committed to tackling the country's serious social crisis and developing effective citizenship.

In 1985, when elections were held only for mayors of state capitals, the PT performed well. It lost by a hair in Goiânia and won, quite unexpectedly, in Fortaleza, the capital of the poor north-eastern state of Ceará. The new mayor was a young woman, Maria Luisa Fontenelle, who obtained 35 per cent of the vote. Three years earlier, the PT candidate for mayor had received less than 1 per cent. It was one of those unexpected developments, later to benefit other PT candidates, in which the PT managed to tap into the profound social discontent of many poor and middle-class voters. As Margaret Keck has shown, the peculiar dynamics of Brazilian politics made the PT the ideal vehicle for the protest vote, the 'last hope for change' of desperate voters. However, as the PT was to find out to its cost, these sporadic spurts in voter support, reflected in freak electoral successes, are highly deceptive. They do not indicate solid, reliable growth in party support, but are merely one-off protests, with most voters returning to the old parties once their rage is spent. As the next chapter shows, Fontenelle's administration was not a success.

* * *

The PT continued to expand in 1985 and 1986, despite unfavourable political circumstances. Tancredo Neves, set to become Brazil's first civilian president for over twenty years, was taken ill on the eve of his inauguration in March 1985 and died before taking office. José Sarney, a right-wing politician made vice-president as a sop to the military, became president. In an effort to win votes, Sarney launched an economic stabilisation package, known as the *Cruzado* plan, in early 1986. The plan ultimately failed, but for eight or nine months it both held down inflation and boosted consumption among the poor. It was immensely popular and, largely as a result, the parties from Sarney's Democratic Alliance (the centrist PMDB and the right-wing PFL) swept the board in the November elections for state governors and for Congress. The electoral potential of an effective anti-inflation plan was clearly demonstrated.

These elections were particularly important, because the new Congress was also to function as a Constituent Assembly, drawing up a new democratic constitution to replace the old authoritarian one by which the military had ruled. The PT had hoped to do well in the elections, enabling it to play a key role in this process. But, deprived of the protest vote, it only managed to double its representation in Congress to 16 federal deputies – by no means an insignificant achievement, but none the less a bitter disappointment to many members. Lula himself did spectacularly well, winning 650,000 votes, more than any other member of Congress. Though the PT's deputies were hopelessly outnumbered in a Congress of 570 members, they were all extremely active, with a cumulative impact on the new Constitution that was quite disproportionate to their voting strength. They succeeded, among other achievements, in extending full labour rights to maids and other domestic workers previously excluded, in increasing paid maternity leave to 120 days, and in broadening the conditions under which it was legal for unions to declare strike action. Their main political innovation was to try and give mass-based organisations a say by encouraging them to collect petitions with hundreds of thousands of signatures calling for amendments to the draft constitution.

Despite his own personal success, Lula on several occasions expressed concern at the energy which the party was expending on elections. In an interview with the PT newspaper, shortly before the election, he commented:

> To tell the truth, we've been putting a lot of energy into elections, and we've been neglecting the nuclei. But a party like the PT needs deep roots in society if it is to win elections, to govern, and to carry out a programme. I still think that the nuclei are the best way of creating a real mass party.

The real breakthrough for the PT came in the municipal elections in November 1988, the last to be held under the old constitution. By then the *Cruzado* plan had collapsed, just as the PT had predicted, and inflation had re-emerged at an annual rate of a thousand per cent, at that point an all-time record. The elections occurred at the end of a wave of strikes, some of

59

which had been violently repressed by the authorities. The army had been sent in to break up a strike by metalworkers at a steel mill in Volta Redonda in the state of Rio, and three workers had been killed. The public was in revolt, and the PT was there to pick up the protest vote.

The PT unexpectedly elected 36 mayors in 12 states, including three state capitals – Vitória, Porto Alegre and, most surprising of all, São Paulo, Brazil's largest city. The success in São Paulo stunned the party, because its candidate, Luiza Erundina, somehow overcame prejudice, deeply entrenched in São Paulo, against both women and north-eastern migrants. Just like Luisa Fontenelle in Fortaleza, Luiza Erundina made huge gains in the final days of the campaign, as the electorate, deeply disillusioned by the collapse of the *Cruzado* plan, suddenly began to believe that Erundina could win. For the first time the PT benefited from tactical voting, as voters opted for Erundina to defeat the extreme right-wing candidate, Paulo Maluf (who later had his revenge by getting himself elected as Erundina's successor, also on the back of some tactical voting). Erundina's victory was widely reported as the greatest shock in Brazil's electoral history.

The scale of the PT's victory should not be exaggerated; Brazil has about 5,000 municipal governments, though many are very small. But by gaining control over such important cities, the PT had for the first time earned a real chance to show that its central message about building up 'popular power' was more than empty rhetoric. The next chapter will look at the use the PT made of this opportunity.

* * *

The volatility of the Brazilian political scene was again evident in 1989, the year in which, for the first time since the military coup in 1964, the country freely elected its president. Though 1989 is recalled with great sadness by many *petistas* for Lula's failure, by a whisker, to win the presidency, it was also a year of extraordinary achievements for the party. For the first time it showed itself able to mobilise the whole country.

The year did not start auspiciously. In the early months a wave of strikes swept through the country, some of them ending in violence. Lula was the only presidential candidate to endorse openly the industrial action and was bitterly attacked by much of the press for provoking 'chaos' and 'disorder'. At the same time, some of the PT's new mayors, including Luiza Erundina, were finding it difficult to reconcile their commitment to revolutionary change with their duty as mayors to the whole population. It was a challenge that all the new incumbents found difficult; the PT expelled five of the 36 mayors from the party for 'betraying PT principles'. None of this helped Lula, and in July opinion polls suggested that he had the support of only six per cent of the population. It seemed that no one, least of all Lula, would be able to stop the front-runner, the flamboyant, articulate and wealthy Fernando Collor de Mello, a little-known former governor of the northeastern state of Alagoas. With the help of Globo television, Collor was running a slick, well-funded television campaign fulminating against the corruption of the politicians in Brasília. Successfully projecting himself as an 'outsider', he was picking up much of the protest vote and was well ahead in the opinion polls.

In September and October, the PT's campaign unexpectedly picked up momentum, as attendance at Lula's rallies soared. A week before the first round of the election, his campaign ended with two huge rallies in São Paulo and Rio de Janeiro, each attracting a quarter of a million people. Even PT activists find the turnaround baffling. Some point to the PT's access, from mid-September, to free electoral time on television. This, they say, helped to make up for the PT's chronic shortage of funds, bringing Lula's message to a part of the electorate that had been difficult to reach earlier in the campaign. Others believe that the months of campaigning, particularly by PT supporters in the Catholic Church, finally paid off. Whatever the reasons, part of the protest vote switched from Collor to Lula.

Under the new electoral regulations, in force for the first time, the election of presidents, state governors and mayors was no longer decided by a simple majority. Unless an absolute majority was obtained by the top contender, a run-off was now required between the two leading candidates. In the first round of the presidential elections, held on 15 November, Collor came comfortably first, with 28 per cent of the votes. Lula just scraped into second place, with 16.5 per cent of the votes, as against 16 per cent for the former governor of Rio, Leonel Brizola. It was a difference of less than 450,000 votes out of a total vote of about 72 million.

The second round was held on 17 December. As polling day approached, huge crowds were attracted to Lula's rallies in a climate of mounting excitement as *petistas* began to smell victory. With the opinion polls suggesting that Lula, on a rising wave of support, would forge into the lead on election day, Collor resorted to dirty tricks. He tracked down Lula's old girlfriend, Miriam Cordeiro, who had borne his daughter, Luriam. Reportedly after a payment of US$23,000, Miriam went on television to claim that Lula had tried to make her have an abortion, a political bombshell in a Catholic country where abortion is still illegal. Lula was deeply shaken, and never regained his confidence.

In the final three-hour televised debate a few days later, Lula failed to show his normal good form. Still shaken by the Miriam incident, Lula was further thrown off balance by an oblique reference by Collor to another more recent affair. Much later, Lula commented, 'It wasn't the Luriam episode in itself which got votes for Collor. What it did was to wage psychological war on me. In my normal state, I could hold 20 debates with Collor, and I'd win 21. It made me lose that advantage.' Globo television then produced a shortened version of the debate, deliberately edited to show Lula at a disadvantage. Later a Globo editor told a reporter from a local newspaper, 'I never did dirtier work in my life.' This version was repeated endlessly on the Globo networks.

A week before the election, a leading businessman was kidnapped by Latin American leftists, mainly Chileans. He was freed by the police and, on the day before the election, television news programmes repeatedly showed shots of heavy-duty weapons and PT electoral propaganda, reportedly found together in the kidnappers' house. No evidence was ever produced of the alleged PT connection, but the PT's image undoubtedly suffered. The election result was close – 35 million votes for Collor, 31 million for Lula – but probably not close enough to have been determined by fraud, as some PT supporters claimed.

* * *

The 1989 presidential campaign highlighted the role of Brazil's media in undermining the PT's electoral prospects. Television and radio are more important in politics in Brazil than in most industrial countries because of the country's widespread illiteracy and low purchasing power. Brazil changed almost overnight from being a non-literate culture with strong oral traditions to a modern radio and TV society. Two out of every three households today have a television set. In shanty towns, TV aerials protrude from nearly every shack. While the rich pay less attention to radio and television, it is through TV and, to a lesser extent, radio, that most of the poor and the middle classes develop their understanding of the world. The military, in power from 1964 to 1982, used the media as a form of social control, resorting to coercion only occasionally. With the return to democracy, the broadcasting media has become even more important, as the ruling élite's sole remaining source of social control.

While in most industrialised countries press freedom is considered a form of defence against abuses of power, the press in Brazil still operates under the 1967 Press Law, passed by the military regime, which, among other repressive clauses, forbids journalists from accusing the president, the heads of the Senate, the Chamber of Deputies or the Supreme Court, heads of foreign states or their representatives in Brazil of any crime and, if they are sued for libel for doing so, forbids them from being able to justify their accusations in court by proving that they are true.

In many countries in the North, radio and television are forbidden by their statutes forbid them from being openly biased in favour of any political party. In Brazil the ruling élite routinely uses television and radio concessions, over which they have a monopoly, as a means of retaining political power. One network alone, TV Globo, dominates the audience and during electoral campaigns openly promotes its preferred candidates. Even in the written media, where government control is less severe, there is little ideological pluralism. All important newspapers are owned by conservative businessmen and follow the same basic ideology.

* * *

The electoral defeat was a serious psychological blow, for the PT had felt victory within its grasp. The following year Lula amazed many members by saying that he had decided not to stand as a federal deputy again, even though he would undoubtedly not only have been elected but, under Brazil's electoral system, attracted enough votes to have taken at least another dozen PT candidates into Congress with him. The decision was bitterly criticised by some groups within the PT, but Lula was adamant. In his four years in the Chamber of Deputies, he had become convinced that most Brazilian politicians were corrupt:

> They are lackeys. They can be bought. They behave in Congress as if it were the stock market and they were traders – they sell their vote to the highest bidder. What we need is to change the behaviour of our politicians, to change our institutions.

He had become so ashamed of being a federal deputy that he used to get up early in the morning to talk to workers at the factory gate at 6am, as a way of convincing them (and himself) that he was still a loyal member of the working class.

Lula was certain that the only way real change could occur would be through strengthening the grassroots of the party, particularly the nuclei, many of which had by then been abandoned by party members who had been putting their energy into electoral committees:

> If the PT ever decides that the nuclei are not essential for its survival, it will be then that its idea for creating a new kind of political party will come to an end. The nucleus is so important that if we abandon it, we lose the very thing that makes the PT different. The PT cannot just discuss politics once every four years, during elections. Any party can do that. Of course, the nucleus is important at election time, but it's essential for other reasons too. For example, where can people talk about politics if they don't have a nucleus at their workplace or in their neighbourhood? When we decided to set up nuclei, it was because we wanted the party to go to the people, not to wait until the people came

to it. It's the only way we have of letting ordinary people – housewives, students, and so on – take part in politics, talk about their everyday problems, about national problems, even international problems. It's the only way that the PT can face up to the economic power of the opposition at election times, and it's also the only way that the PT can prevent a clampdown by big economic groups or by the military. If we're organised at the grassroots, whether at the workplace or in the neighbourhood, then I don't think that any military coup can put an end to us.

Lula decided to spend much of the next four years travelling extensively throughout Brazil. It was an idea that later germinated into his five *caravanas*, long trips throughout Brazil in which he covered 40,000 kilometres. His aim was two-fold: to take the PT's message to areas of the country where the PT's presence was weak and to prepare for government by getting to know personally the problems faced by ordinary Brazilians in all the different regions of the country.

Collor came to office in March 1990. Within days he announced a spectacular economic adjustment plan that, among other measures, confiscated billions of dollars in individual savings as part of a radical strategy for ending inflation. 'I'll only be allowed one shot at the monster, inflation', he said in a phrase that he must have later regretted, 'so it had better be lethal.'

* * *

But lethal it was not. Inflation re-emerged, gradually at first, and then with increasing impetus. Soon Collor was in trouble on another front. In May 1992 came the first evidence that he was involved in corruption on an unparalleled scale. Once again, the PT was in its element, pressing for Congressional enquiries and organising large anti-Collor demonstrations. News magazines, particularly the influential weekly, *Veja*, no longer fettered by authoritarian censorship, carried out some fine investigative journalism. Although Globo television was slow to join in, the usual constraints on the media were less in evidence.

Collor, it seemed, had alienated the traditional centres of power and patronage. Arriving in Brasília from the north-east with his own entourage of advisers, he had not respected the old rules of the game. Now, as he came under attack, few veteran politicians sprang to his defence, though none can have wished the investigations to go as far as they did. For weeks the televised proceedings of the Congressional enquiry were watched by millions of amazed Brazilians. Collor's henchman, PC Farias, had, it emerged, headed a veritable state within a state. Millions of dollars had changed hands, as large companies had not only paid 'PC' hefty commissions to win inflated contracts, but had also bribed federal deputies to allocate huge sums of money to phantom projects. Corruption, it became apparent, had become the chief purpose of government. Lula's allegations about corruption in Congress seemed fully justified.

With a vast amount of evidence stacked against him, Collor resigned from office on 31 December 1992, just hours before he would have been impeached by Congress. Even though he no longer held office, Congress decided, perhaps unconstitutionally, to strip him of his political rights for eight years.

* * *

Just as after the death of Tancredo, the vice-president took over. This time it was the erratic, hot-tempered Itamar Franco. Following in Sarney's footsteps, he procrastinated, squandering the groundswell of support gained in replacing the highly unpopular Collor. With the opinion polls giving Lula a steady 25 per cent level of support among the electorate, far ahead of any other potential candidate, the PT believed it had a real chance of winning power.

The 1993 National Meeting, held in June to mark the start of the presidential campaign, drew up an ambiguous manifesto. It approved two basic ideas: firstly, that the party should propose a long programme of deep-rooted structural reforms to uproot social injustice and secondly, that this should be done within the capitalist system, by building a broad political coalition under PT hegemony. The campaign was not defined simply as an electoral dispute to win the presidency but as a strategic step, 'the point of departure for a democratic and popular movement capable of unifying wide sectors of the population around the banner of structural reform', according to the conference resolutions. Winning the presidency was not seen as the seizure of power, nor even as an end in itself, but as a key stage in making workers the hegemonic force in Brazilian society.

'Social apartheid' was placed at the centre of the 1994 election campaign. The manifesto stated that over sixty million Brazilians lived in poverty, 32 million of them in absolute poverty. It claimed it was possible to engage society in a new model of development that would still be capitalist in essence but would create millions of jobs, incorporate the poor into the consumer market, distribute wealth, and preserve the environment. Creating a mass market in Brazil was the core aim outlined in the manifesto.

Notable by its absence was any specific reference to the vexed question of hyperinflation, then running at 33 per cent a month, even though it was precisely the poor who were worst hit by almost daily price rises. It also should have been clear that high inflation had to be eliminated before any programme of structural reform could be successfully undertaken. Yet the

PT, in a strategic error that was to do it much harm, failed to address this problem. There seems to have been two reasons for this. First of all, the PT found it difficult to deal with any economic concept that was not in the classic Marxist dictionary. Secondly, the party still had a working-class mentality, born out of decades of wage bargaining, which found it impossible to imagine that a national agreement between employers and the government for eliminating inflation could serve the interests of workers. So the National Meeting demanded, instead, monthly wage increases, failing to see that this would merely feed inflation in a self-defeating spiral.

* * *

Even so, by early 1994 it seemed that nothing could prevent Lula from becoming Brazil's next president. He was spending much of his time travelling all over the country in the *caravanas* and was increasingly convinced that only a PT government could find a way of resolving the country's horrific social crisis, which he was discovering was even worse than he had imagined.

The first *caravana* went to the north-east. Driven by an inexhaustible passion to find out what was going on in the region, Lula and his wife, Marisa, set an inexorable pace. Near the beginning of the trip, José Genoíno, a leading member of Congress who, as a former guerrilla fighter, was no stranger to physical hardship, could bear it no longer, 'Lula, it can't go on like this. Here we are, at three o'clock in the afternoon, and we still haven't had lunch. We are campaigning against hunger, not in favour of it!'

The group witnessed extraordinary scenes. Travelling in the barren hinterland, ravaged by one of its periodic droughts, Lula held a meeting on a hilltop, by a large cross. His audience were ragged, half-starved peasant farmers who had travelled from miles around to hear him. The first woman to come forward to speak held everyone spellbound. One of those present wrote afterwards, 'Her vocabulary was as sparse as the vegetation in this barren area where nothing is wasted. Her grammar was as dilapidated as her clothes and was at times as difficult to fathom as the sense behind their lives. But that speech, particularly her aggressive use of irony, left everyone astounded. I doubt if any politician alive today could articulate his thoughts as powerfully. Everyone, even journalists, were impressed by the force and the dignity of her voice. It belonged to a short, 32-year old woman, with nine children, who was the colour of an Indian and had the ferocity of a Mother Courage. The woman, Maria do Socorro Lira Feitosa, told the story of her community, a story of poverty, unemployment and hunger.'

When they knew that the *caravana* was passing nearby, Socorro and a hundred others from her community had wrapped up a little manioc flour in palm leaves, gathered together some candles and set off at eleven o'clock at night to walk the 48km to the meeting place. Early the next morning, they had passed through a small town, the centre of the local government, but the mayor had refused to see them. After telling the PT what she and her companions wanted for their community, Socorro demanded food and transport home. A delegation from the PT *caravana*, including Eduardo Suplicy, at that time the PT's only senator, went with Socorro back to the town. The mayor, embarrassed by the presence of a senator, had little choice but to provide 200 bread rolls for Socorro and her companions and arrange some trucks to take them home. The PT helped with the expenditure.

Everywhere he went, Lula learnt more. After his trip by boat and by jeep to small communities in the Amazon forest, Lula commented, 'This *caravana* to the Amazon has been a lesson in life for me. However often I might have gone to Belém or Manaus, I wouldn't have found out what the lives of most of the people in this region were like. I had no idea how difficult it was for people just to survive, even though we're nearly at the end of the 20th Century. At times, it seems that some of these people are living in the 16th Century and watching Globo television from the 21st Century. These *caravanas* mean that for a while we can change our behaviour as political leaders. Instead of speaking all the time, we can try to listen.'

At times, during this same trip to the Amazon, among uneducated people with a deep, mystical belief in Christianity, Lula dared to say things that would have been misinterpreted in the south. In the town of Obidos beside the Amazon river, he said to a crowd, 'Imagine if Christ came back to earth today. Imagine if he looked around him now, as he looked around 2,000 years ago and decided what needed to be done... What would he have been called? ... A communist, a communist.' He then explained that Christ would have been called this because he wanted respect for the poor, equality and food for everyone and went on, 'It was for this reason that they crucified him. If he were among us today, those who call me a communist would have said the same about him, "This fellow's a communist. We have to get rid of him".'

In the street markets and ports, Lula blended in to the crowd. Several journalists noticed that people did not treat him like a typical politician, asking for personal favours or money. Instead, they demanded more jobs in the region, lower prices for staple foods, a better transport system. Lula always gave them the same kind of reply, 'No individual, not even a political party, can give you solutions to your problems. The only way things will change is if mass-based organisations start controlling governments, if we reverse the relationship between those who govern and those who are governed.'

Lula always encouraged people in the crowds to talk. One morning, during the *caravana* to the south of the country, he was in the main square of the town of São Luis Gonzaga in Rio Grande do Sul. He decided to give the microphone to the crowd and spotted a man who had lost the ends of his fingers on his right hand. Lula, who had himself lost part of a finger in a factory accident, thought that the man must have been through something similar on a worse scale. He asked him his name. 'Ari Marim Vieira,' came the reply. 'How did you lose your fingers?' 'I'm a chicken thief, and the owner caught me.' General laughter. One of Lula's companions commented, 'All the time we're finding out in the press and on televison about the budget thieves, stealing millions while pretending to be honest deputies. Long live the sincerity of our chicken thief!'

Lula loved the contact with ordinary people. He could tell jokes that he couldn't tell at the big rallies in the urban centres, for they would have offended the middle classes. Raising guffaws of laughter, he said on one occasion, 'The ruling classes have their eyes turned towards Europe and their bums turned towards Brazil.' Often he would come away from these meetings with tears in his eyes.

* * *

Lula came back from these trips ever more determined to use his term of office to help the poor. He was surging ahead in the opinion polls. By May he had the support of almost forty per cent of the population, more than twice that received by any other candidate. Everyone, not just the *petistas*, believed that Lula was heading for certain victory. Though Lula fought against it, a triumphalist note crept into his campaign. Some *petistas*, thinking that victory was already theirs, put less energy into campaigning compared to 1989. Though Lula himself favoured an alliance with a breakaway faction of the Social Democrats, radical groups within the PT, confident that Lula would win on his own, vetoed the deal.

The PT, however, had underestimated the tenacity with which the Brazilian Right clings to power. Aware that it could not get one of its own candidates elected, Brazil's biggest right-wing party, the Liberal Front Party (PFL) formed an alliance with the Social Democrats (PSDB), even supporting their candidate, the former Marxist and renowned left-wing intellectual, Fernando Henrique Cardoso, for the presidency. The first move made by the hastily-assembled anti-Lula front was to appropriate the PT's manifesto. All the principal targets, including creating eight million jobs, the programme to encourage small businesses and the land reform programme, were incorporated into the conservative camp's manifesto. They had evidently decided that social reform had strong electoral appeal and had to be neutralised.

The anti-Lula front, in alliance with the Itamar Franco government, then moved to transform conditions within the country in order to strengthen

Fernando Henrique's bid for the presidency. Earlier in the year, as Finance Minister, Fernando Henrique had launched an economic stabilisation programme. The original intention had been to carry out a wide range of painful economic and political reforms to pave the way for the introduction much later on of a new stable currency. However, aware that the only part of the programme that would win votes would be the introduction of a stable currency, the anti-Lula front reversed the order of the measures. It brought forward the introduction of the new currency, the *Real*, to 1 July to achieve the maximum political impact on the election. The *Real* plan, as the stabilisation package was known, was particularly Machiavellian, in that Cardoso first allowed inflation to rise from about 25 per cent a month to nearly 50 per cent. This increased dramatically both the initial desperation of the poor who, without the protection of indexed bank accounts, suffered a fearful decline in their standard of living, and then their enormous relief, when finally the new stable currency was introduced.

To reinforce the impact of the plan, Fernando Henrique played his part in the nationwide anti-Lula campaign. At times, this meant that the former Marxist, who as a sociologist had made scathing attacks on Brazil's corrupt and authoritarian political élites, had to align himself openly with the Right. His embarrassment sometimes showed, despite all his efforts to hide it. Worst of all for him were the obligatory trips to the north-east, as the guest of the old political party bosses, known as the *coronéis* (colonels). There, he had to go through all the antics of populist politics. In Alagoas, he had to take a ride on a donkey which, with the ignorance of an urban, middle-class intellectual, he called a horse. In Bahia, he had to let the local politicians dress him up in a cowboy jacket, made out of real cowhide. In Pernambuco, he was the guest of the Coelho family, a powerful local clan. The first member of the family to arrive in the region was Coronel Clementino de Souza Coelho. He laid claim to a huge area of land and later became an important shareholder in a steel mill and a hydroelectric project. Nilo Coelho, the most ambitious of his eight sons, became president of the Senate and governor of the state. He and his brothers had a key role in setting up the so-called 'drought industry', a rich gravy train bringing milllions of dollars into the region, allegedly to combat drought, but in practice to line the pockets of local landowners.

What did the Coelho clan think of Fernando Henrique? 'When he realises that we are serious people, when he gets to know us properly, when he feels at home with us, then he is going to give up all this social democracy nonsense and come over to our side,' said the current head of the clan, Osvaldo Coelho. And Fernando Henrique? 'What did Osvaldo Coelho do? All the time I was with him, he kept telling me that the region needed water, schools, energy. How can I be against all that?' And later, 'You don't achieve anything without the support of people like him. If you say,

"I'm not going to have anything do with him", then you shouldn't go into politics. You have to have two things – strength and will-power. It's only then that society changes.'

It was evident, for those who wanted to see it, that the stabilisation plan had been completely restructured to get Fernando Henrique elected. André Lara Resende, one of the plan's main architects, was quite honest about this: 'We're here to get Fernando Henrique elected. That's what it's all about. The real stabilisation of the economy will take from three to five years.' This analysis was supported by the news magazine, *Veja*, 'Gradually we've been hearing less and less about fiscal adjustment, constitutional reform, privatisation. All that's left is the new currency. This means, in fact, that what should have been the last phase of the plan – the new currency – has been turned into its point of departure. The most difficult part of the plan has been left for the next president.'

Despite this, most of the media was quite happy to go along with the government's plans. Among other mud-slinging efforts, the media claimed that Lula admired Hitler, that he had become a 'professional politician', and that he grown rich. It reported his views on abortion and homosexuality in a distorted manner to alarm Catholics and to anger evangelicals. 'They made Fernando Henrique the prince and Lula the frog,' recalls Lula's wife, Marisa. The PT was described as a radical party, dominated by radicals, and falsely accused of receiving money from the Brazilian underworld, foreign political parties and even the Italian Mafia.

Cardoso also had the government machine behind him. PT supporters were vaguely aware that the population was being manipulated, but were powerless to combat TV Globo's huge and efficient propaganda machine. Then, in one of those extraordinary eruptions that from time to time occur in Brazilian politics, a private conversation between Cardoso's successor as Finance Minister, Rubens Rícupero, and a high-level TV Globo executive, as they sat waiting in a TV studio, was accidentally broadcast on cable television. Rícupero, whose lean, ascetic face and kind, fatherly demeanour, had given him a monk-like public image, candidly admitted that he was concealing unfavourable economic statistics, explaining, 'I have no scruples. I take full advantage of the good figures, the bad ones I hide.' He boasted of the help he was giving Cardoso:

> Just between you and me, so as not to sound boastful, [Cardoso] needs me more than I need him ... Countless people have written to me saying that they are going to vote for him because of me, and he knows it. Today I'm his main electoral asset.

Rícupero chatted casually about the arrangements for getting him on the *Fantástico* show, TV Globo's highly popular all-day variety programme that goes out to huge audiences on Sundays.

As the interview had been seen by several hundred people throughout the country, the gaffe could not be covered up. Rícupero resigned, giving a powerful press interview in which he broke down in tears, and, as if at confession, begged forgiveness for his boastfulness and pride. Little mention was made of what to many in the PT seemed a much more important issue – the close links between TV Globo and the government. For a few days Cardoso dropped slightly in the opinion polls, but he soon recovered. Few ordinary Brazilians knew what the word 'scruples' meant, and the mass media were not about to enlighten them. Fernando Henrique's candidacy went from strength to strength. On 3 October, he was elected president in the first round, winning 54 per cent of the vote. Lula trailed home with just 27 per cent.

* * *

Lula's defeat, though a bitter disappointment to the PT, should not perhaps have come as a complete surprise. Through the introduction of the *Real* plan, Cardoso brought optimism back into the political arena. People began to believe in the future and to hope that the government's plan would work. Much of the protest vote collapsed, leaving the PT with the support only of the committed. In 1989, shortly after his defeat in that year's presidential contest, Lula had warned against excessive optimism:

> The fact that we received so much support in the election doesn't mean we will enjoy the same position in the next elections. The fact that we received all those votes doesn't mean we have the structure to maintain that level of support. It's important to remember that, though I received 31 million votes in the second round, the PT's vote was, in fact, the twelve million that I got in the first round. We received almost triple that in the second round, owing to the alliances we built.

Many *petistas* attribute their defeat to the gullibility of Brazilian voters, whose reaction they see as particularly inexplicable since they had already been taken in by the 1986 *Cruzado* stabilisation plan. That plan had been an enormous success for the first six months, but then, to the bitter resentment of most Brazilians, collapsed just days after the election, making it clear that it had been artificially sustained to allow the government to win votes.

This explanation, however, is simplistic. It is true that, just as in 1986, the Brazilian public was manipulated by the government in 1994; Cardoso's economic stabilisation package was deliberately restructured to win him the presidency. The timing of the introduction of the new currency, the *Real*, was even more blatant than in the case of the *Cruzado*. When they were introduced, however, both plans were also genuine attempts to resolve the country's prolonged economic crisis. The *Cruzado* plan was ruined by

President Sarney's insistence on squeezing out of it every ounce of political capital. The jury is still out on whether or not the *Real* plan has also been destroyed by excessive political manipulation. Much will depend on Cardoso's ability, after delivering an extraordinarily optimistic message during the electoral campaign, to insist now on the painful parts of the economic stabilisation programme, such as fiscal and constitutional reform, privatisation and the restructuring of the state, that he largely ignored during the campaign.

* * *

There are other quite different reasons for Lula's defeat. Despite his efforts to reassure the wealthy, the PT's proposal for tackling social apartheid seems to have scared away some voters, particularly the upper-middle classes. One of the problems seems to have been that the proposal, particularly the way it was delivered by Lula, seemed to benefit only the poorest sectors of the population. In the way Lula uses it, the very term 'social apartheid' is a moral concept, not an economic one. Lula, brought up in a very poor family, is deeply marked by his past. He cannot accept any proposal that ignores the plight of the destitute, nor can he think with the detachment and abstraction of a general drawing up a war plan, who takes it for granted that there will be casualties.

Lula's view of the world was reinforced by the *caravanas* he undertook in 1993 and 1994. Coming face to face with unbearable poverty, he became more committed than ever to improving the lot of the very poor. This is an admirable human quality, but at times it comes across as something of an obsession, a denunciation of the evils of the present system, rather than a positive proposal on how to move forward. Such an approach may have alienated the average family, which, although poor, has a roof over its head, eats regularly, sends its children to school and does not like being identified with the destitute.

At the same time, just by looking at him, any Brazilian can tell that Lula comes from a poor family. This and his somewhat illiterate (though extraordinarily powerful) way of speaking were exploited by the media. Though progress is slowly being made in overcoming the prejudice felt by the poor against the idea of being governed by one of their own, it is still an important obstacle to a PT victory.

Despite Lula's concern for the destitute, the PT's institutional links with them are weaker than with the merely poor. In recent years, not just in Brazil but throughout Latin America, many destitute families have been attracted to the highly conservative Protestant evangelical churches, to which they devote all their allegiance, becoming activists of the Right and on some occasions fighting the Left in fanatical fashion. About 16 per cent of the Brazilian population now belongs to these sects. It is less than in Guatemala or Chile but, even so, a very large group of people. The evangelical churches give their followers a code of conduct and a set of values with which to distinguish themselves from the people around them, particularly the criminal gangs that control the shanty towns. They also set up self-help networks just as the Muslim fundamentalists do, with the same success. The evangelical lobby against the PT was second only to the stabilisation plan in accounting for Lula's defeat. Furthermore, as the Catholic Church hierarchy has realized that it has been losing ground to the evangelicals, it has been guiding the Church away from politics back to a narrower and more mystical view of religion, weakening its commitment to liberation theology and damaging the PT. In several areas of the country under Catholic Church influence, veteran PT activists with Church backgrounds failed to be re-elected. The weakening of its Catholic base poses a serious challenge for the PT's future development.

Even so, the election results were not the unmitigated disaster for the PT that press reports have suggested both in Brazil and abroad. Though the PT remains a minority force in Congress, it has increased by almost half its number of federal deputies and elected five senators, compared with just one in 1990 (see Table 4). Lula, too, gained five million more first round votes in 1994 that he had in 1989. The PT has undoubtedly continued its rapid growth.

The party's sporadic appeal in times of crisis has tempted some party activists into believing that there is a short-cut to political power. But, as we shall discuss in the next chapter, such a route, though seductive, might be harmful to the party's long-term project of creating 'popular power' in Brazil.

Table 4   National Vote for the PT in Congressional Elections

	% of votes	No. of seats in Chamber of Deputies	No. of seats in Senate
1982	1.8	8	0
1986	3.2	16	0
1990	7	35	1
1994	9	49	5

Table 5   The Distribution of Seats in Congress in 1995

Party	Chamber	Senate	Total
PMDB	110	21	131
PFL	91	19	110
PSDB	63	11	74
PPR	52	6	58
PT	49	5	54
Others	148	19	167
Totals	513	81	594

Table 6: Presidential Election Results, 1989 and 94

1989	Votes (million)	% of votes
Round One		
Fernando Collor	20	28
Lula	12	16.5
Leonel Brizola	11.5	16
Round Two		
Fernando Collor	35	49
Lula	31	43
1994		
Fernando Henrique Cardoso	34	54
Lula	17	27

6
A Taste of Power:
the PT in Local Government

Although the results of the 1982 elections fell well short of the expectations of many *petistas*, the PT elected two mayors. One was of a tiny town in the interior of the backward state of Maranhão in the northeast, where, unbeknown to the PT's national executive, a left-wing priest had put together a PT slate. As no other opposition party was represented in the elections, it was voted into office by an electorate largely composed of poor rural workers. Under intense pressure from the traditional party bosses who ran the region, the mayor and other PT councillors resigned after a few months in office.

The other victory was much more significant, occurring in the large industrial town of Diadema on the outskirts of São Paulo. Diadema had scarcely existed in 1950, with a population of just 3,000, but as thousands of migrants from the north-east had poured into São Paulo in the following decades, its population had soared, reaching 230,000 by 1980. The migrants squatted illegally on public or private land, building their own shacks as near as possible to the factories where they hoped to find work. Diadema was situated near the somewhat older industrial towns of Santo André, São Bernardo and São Caetano, the famous ABC region which had been the birthplace of the PT. Its rapid expansion led the local inhabitants to add another letter, making it the ABCD region.

Diadema's inhabitants suffered all the hardships associated with rapid, chaotic and disorderly urbanisation. About a third of them lived in shanty towns, where raw sewage stagnated in pools; infant mortality was almost twice as high as in the neighbouring towns; fewer children went to school, as they had to work from an early age to supplement the family income. It was just the kind of town which the 'new unionists' had dreamed of winning when they set up the PT. Yet the PT's victory was unexpected. Partly because the town had grown so quickly, mass-based organisations were weak. Voters opted for the PT because of the party's high prestige in the region as a whole, not because the party was strongly rooted in the town.

The new mayor, Gilson Menezes, was himself a migrant from the north-east. At 12 years old he had gone out to work, becoming a metalworker at 18. He had been one of the organisers of the 1978 wave of strikes and had helped found the PT. He won the election by just 678 votes, benefiting from a three-way split that divided votes almost equally between the PT and two established parties.

Once in office, Gilson Menezes wanted to govern with the aid of 'popular councils', as PT orthodoxy demanded. These councils, made up of representatives of mass-based organisations, would set the agenda for the municipal government. But Gilson found it difficult to make this arrangement work in practice, particularly since Diadema had so few effective mass-based organisations. In recent years the PT had started building them, but it was a slow process and Gilson could not wait that long. Instead, he started to create his own 'mass-based organisations' in poor sectors of the town, behaving much like the old-style populist politicians who had always been condemned by the PT. Furthermore, the PT, not expecting to win, had failed to carry out any in-depth study of the city's problems, making it much harder to structure consultation with the groups that were to benefit from its actions. Gilson ended up abandoning the idea of setting up 'popular councils', disappointing many PT members.

Another problem, which returned to haunt later PT administrations, was how to organise relations between the local PT directorate and the municipal governments. After a great deal of wrangling, the new mayor won the right to appoint staff in whom he had confidence, without consulting the local party. But the in-fighting caused ill-will, with the party objecting in particular to Gilson's decision to appoint his close friend and former union colleague, Juracy Magalhães, as his chief of staff.

The new government faced severe financial constraints. Forty per cent of its budget went to repay debts of past administrations and another fifty per cent on the wages of municipal employees, leaving only ten per cent for investment or new initiatives.

Despite all these setbacks, real progress was made. In an important attempt to promote *transparência* (openness) in public accounts, the party went to poor neighbourhoods and held open meetings, explaining how it spent its budget. It also did all it could to bring down the price of public transport, knowing how much of a burden it was for poor families. The planning department refused to accept the reasons given by the largest bus company for increasing fares. In public hearings it demonstrated that, according to the figures collected, the fare should be reduced, rather than increased. Diadema ended up with the lowest bus fare in the region. The company also had to agree to put new buses on the much-travelled routes to São Bernardo. In the following year, the municipal council persuaded the company to issue free bus-passes outside rush-hour for pensioners and the unemployed, an initiative later copied in many other parts of the country.

The most controversial programme undertaken by the municipal government was to provide urban services to the shanty towns. It persuaded the

São Paulo state water and sewage company to provide electricity and running water to any shanty town whose inhabitants were prepared to build roads at least four metres wide. This was not as easy as it sounded, for it meant that in the overcrowded conditions of the shanty towns, some shacks had to be relocated. It was, however, an important exercise in community involvement and the whole programme was a great success.

One of the unforeseen consequences was that the programme encouraged homeless families from outside the town to squat illegally on private or public land in Diadema, in the hope that they would receive the same favourable treatment. It was a problem that other PT municipal governments were to face in later years and it divided the party. Gilson and his chief of staff favoured tough action to stop the proliferation of shanty towns, whereas his planning department wanted to handle the problem through the recently formed Municipal Commission of Shanty-town Dwellers.

Eventually, this and other conflicts led most of the officials from the highly successful planning department to resign from the government, accusing Gilson, and more specifically Juracy Magalhães, of clientelism.

The wrangling within the party came to a head in 1985, when the press reported that Juracy and other municipal employees had faked a car accident in order to obtain insurance money to cover previous damage. Despite all the negative publicity, PT leaders insisted on a serious investigation, and Juracy was sacked. It was a painful lesson for Lula and other union leaders. Because many of them, including Lula, had worked with Gilson and Juracy in the São Bernardo and Diadema Metalworkers' Union, they had tended to ignore evidence that something was seriously wrong in the administration. As Margaret Keck has shown in her book *The Workers' Party and Democratization in Brazil*, the main problem, which remained unresolved throughout Diadema's first administration, was the relationship between the party, the municipal government and mass-based organisations.

Despite the divisions and bad press, the PT won the next municipal election in Diadema and won again in 1992, although by then Gilson Menezes had left the party to run on a rival slate. Opinion polls have repeatedly shown that over seventy per cent of the population believe the municipal government to be 'good' or 'very good'. Diadema can legitimately call itself the most *petista* town in Brazil.

The 1985 elections for mayor in the state capitals gave the PT another chance to run a large town, when Maria Luisa Fontenelle unexpectedly won the election in Fortaleza, the capital of the north-eastern state of Ceará, but serious bouts of internal wrangling soon broke out. Fontenelle belonged to a Maoist faction within the PT, which did not enjoy the support of the rest of the party. She was also viciously attacked by local businessmen and landowners, who used every means at their disposal to undermine her government. Because she was separated from her husband, they even went as far as digging holes in the streets and putting broomsticks in them, bearing the crude sexist message, 'This is Maria Luisa's hole in which everyone puts his stick.'

To compound the problems, Fontenelle did not run an efficient administration, failing to provide adequate urban services, such as rubbish collection. This left her government open to attack from the local media, which in turn exacerbated the in-fighting in the party. The PT eventually expelled Fontenelle, who joined the small Brazilian Socialist Party (PSB). From the PT's perspective, the whole experience was a débâcle.

* * *

In 1988 the PT leapt to national prominence, winning the election for mayor in three out of the four ABCD towns and taking Brazil's largest city (São Paulo), two other state capitals (Porto Alegre and Vitória) and several medium-sized towns, including the port of Santos. Altogether some 15 million Brazilians, about ten per cent of the population, came under local PT rule. By 1988, the party was far more aware of the pitfalls of power than it had been six years earlier, when it had first won Diadema, and the dominant mood in the PT national meeting, called just after the results were announced, was of apprehension, in contrast to the euphoria of the *petistas* dancing in the streets of São Paulo.

The PT leaders knew that they had tapped the protest vote, gaining support from people who were not committed *petistas*. These floating voters would not readily give the PT a second chance, unless the party could show that its new-style politics, based on anti-corruption, transparency, honesty and popular participation, could yield concrete results, improving the standard of living of the mass of the population. The sectarian battles that had done so much harm in Diadema and Fortaleza must not be repeated. To help prevent the in-fighting, the PT clarified the remit of its mayors and councillors, agreeing that those elected to office had to carry out the general lines of the party's programme, but were also to be accountable to the needs and interests of everyone in the municipality and were not to be controlled, on a day-to-day basis, by the local PT office.

São Paulo was the most daunting challenge yet faced by the PT. The city has the third largest budget in the country, after the federal government and São Paulo state. It covers an area of 1,500 square kilometres, with a population of 9.5 million, of whom two million live in slums and one million in shanty towns. Another 2.5 million people live on plots of lands that they occupied illegally during the city's rapid and chaotic expansion in the 1950s and 1960s, when tens of thousands of migrants arrived each month from the north-east.

The new mayor of São Paulo was Luiza Erundina, a short, stocky woman with a direct and likeable manner. A migrant from the north-east, she had spent many years as a social worker in the poor eastern part of the city. She had been a founder member of the PT and was linked to its radical left wing. Although her nomination had been opposed by the mainstream of the party, including Lula, she had won by mobilising the support of both the Left and the grassroots. While the PT party machine reluctantly accepted her nomination, it showed no enthusiasm for her candidacy. Party activists recall that a large part of the *Articulação* did not take part in a single rally in her campaign and few big PT names joined in the celebrations after her victory. Some feared that her administration might turn out to be an embarrassing fiasco that would do the party serious damage.

When Erundina took over, the city was bankrupt, with a public debt of US$1.5 billion and closed creches, schools and hospitals. She decided that she could do little without first sorting out the mess. Her administration spent the first year putting its finances in order, rescheduling debts and streamlining the administrative apparatus. It was an option that bore results in the long term, but brought few immediate political gains. The media hounded her, complaining about litter in the streets, poor rubbish collection, the proliferation of street vendors, potholes in the roads and illegal land occupations. She was also accused by members of her own party of being 'technocratic' and of not getting her government moving. By the end of the first year, almost eighty per cent of the city's inhabitants expressed disapproval of her administration.

Lula continued to defend Erundina in public, but her relations with the party head office sank to an all-time low. Angry words were exchanged when Lula lost the second round of the presidential election in December 1989, a year and a half after Erundina took office, partly because of his disappointing performance in São Paulo. The clashes carried on in 1990 and 1991 and it seemed to some observers that, for all the party's talk about learning from the Fortaleza debacle, an irreversible break might occur, with Erundina being forced out of the party.

To the surprise of many of her supporters, Erundina turned out to be a highly pragmatic mayor. Two of her early decisions were particularly unexpected. Claiming that it was an important cultural relic, she expropriated, with compensation, one of the last remaining mansions built in the 19th century by coffee plantation owners. She also negotiated a deal with Shell to build a Formula One racing track. Both measures were well-received by São Paulo's inhabitants, but they did not please the PT local office, which thought that she was pandering to the wishes of the middle classes at the expense of the poor.

Once her finances were in order, Erundina was able to set her priorities, which clearly lay with the poor citizens of the city. As soon as she had funds available, she upgraded school dinners, aware from her years as a social worker that for thousands of children they were the main meal of the day. According to Margaret Keck, Erundina remembers a child who ran away screaming when she first saw a piece of meat on her plate during a school lunch; she thought an animal had got into her food.

She attempted other major initiatives. Before coming to office, she had said that public transport would be a priority, promising both lower fares and a better service, but it proved difficult to honour these commitments in practice. The municipal government had inherited a bankrupt state bus company, with 800 of its 3,300 buses stuck in the garages, awaiting repair. When Erundina's unpopularity was at its height, dozens of buses were wrecked by angry passengers in a near riot. At the outset, the new mayor had hoped to introduce free transport, covering costs by a massive increase on corporation property tax. Not surprisingly, the conservative Municipal Chamber, with which Erundina was constantly at odds, threw out the bill, refusing even to debate it. Erundina, who had anticipated this, hoped to whip up public support, holding huge demonstrations that would force the councillors to rethink, but with support for the PT at a low ebb, the mobilisation never materialised. It was an overwhelming defeat for the PT.

Instead, 50 private companies moved into the vacuum, running 1,500 buses and charging whatever they liked, while the state bus company was forced to cut costs, sacking 3,000 employees. The move was bitterly opposed by the powerful transport union, which had expected unequivocal support from Erundina, a long-time union activist. But as mayor of São Paulo, Erundina had to reconcile the demands of the strikers with the public interest, and she took what the strikers regarded as an unacceptably tough line in the negotiations. The city's bus service was paralysed for nine days, and 800 buses were wrecked by angry strikers. Relations between Erundina and the local PT office sank to their lowest point.

As Erundina was the first to admit, she learnt by trial and error, adapting policies that, while sounding good in theory, failed to work out in practice. She changed her mind over the issue of popular councils, which she had at first enthusiastically endorsed, arguing that they should be deliberative, not just advising the administration, but actually deciding policies for their own sector.

In practice, it turned out to be virtually impossible to run a city of nearly ten million people in this way. The city administration had limited funds and each popular council wanted as much money as possible for its own sector. In the ensuing negotiations, the stronger councils became much more effective in obtaining resources, but none of them was defending the overall interests of the city and its inhabitants. Erundina began to change her mind, saying on several occasions that the system of popular councils was still 'precarious' and that she had to govern in the interests of the majority. In the end, she decided to change the role of the councils, making them consultative rather than deliberative bodies. Her decision disappointed some PT members who had seen the councils as the ultimate and authentic expression of direct local democracy.

Despite the difficulties and disappointments, the administration made some important advances, particularly during its last two years. According to a a study by Fiona Macauley, the achievements were particularly significant in public health, education and housing. Five new hospitals were built and 137 health units enlarged and renovated. A large number of ambulances and radio communication units were bought, and the waiting time for patients calling out the emergency services was cut from 40 to 12 minutes. The number of children going to municipal schools rose by twenty per cent and truancy and failure rates dropped. Conditions for teachers improved considerably, and the outlay on schools' running costs increased five-fold. Some 44 new creches were opened, along with over 300 youth centres and 14 community centres, with six especially designed for the homeless.

When the PT took over, São Paulo had a shortfall of one million houses. With limited resources, the PT could not hope to solve the problem overnight, but it made a start. It built (or started building) 40,000 houses, many of them constructed through a self-build scheme run jointly by the municipal government and community housing groups. Though inadequate, it was a huge building programme, far more ambitious than any previous scheme. The PT also brought water and sanitation to 25,000 families in shanty towns.

The administration made advances in less traditional areas of social policy. New parks were built and a rubbish recycling scheme introduced. Marilena Chauí, the highly respected philosophy professor at the University of São Paulo, was appointed Secretary for Culture and began making the city's cultural activities more accessible to the whole population. She appointed cultural outreach workers to work with local neighbourhood committees; library buses were set up and children's play schemes were established. A summer sports scheme, reaching 320,000 people a day, was introduced. Street sellers, who had previously suffered harassment from the police, shopkeepers and protection rackets, were licensed.

Relations between the council and the PT party structure improved somewhat. After the first difficult year, a new political council was created, bringing together high-level representatives of the municipal administration, the PT's representation in the Municipal Chamber and the PT's local and national offices. It became a forum where difficulties could be discussed and areas of competence delimited. Even so, acrimonious rows continued, particularly between the city administration and the PT's representation in the Municipal Chamber. Relations with some sectors of the business community also improved, as the administration's commitment to sorting out its finances and its unquestionable honesty won grudging respect. Difficulties persisted however, with other business groups, particularly the *Tribunal Municipal de Contas*, an unelected and unaccountable body of five highly-paid 'judges', whose function is to check the city's accounts. The *Tribunal* repeatedly rejected the PT's accounts on technicalities.

There were other problems too. The administration depended heavily on funding from the São Paulo state and federal governments. This has traditionally encouraged clientelism, with funds being passed on as a political favour, rather than by right. At politically sensitive moments Erundina and other PT mayors all over the country found themselves starved of funds. In response, the PT and other parties set up the National Front of Mayors (*Frente Nacional de Prefeitos*) to lobby for the swift and automatic disbursement of funds.

The PT administration was also plagued by legal actions, as opponents sought to block the PT's reforms through the courts. Erundina herself was issued with over a hundred writs, many of which have still not been resolved. One senior member of her staff was sentenced to 18 months' imprisonment for providing a municipal vehicle to take representatives to a meeting of the National Front of Mayors in Brasília.

Not surprisingly, Erundina and her team left office exhausted. Surveys in 1992 showed that São Paulo voters warmly appreciated the improvements in municipal services, but paradoxically continued to have a poor opinion of Erundina and her staff, probably because of the virulent anti-PT coverage in the press. The PT's candidate for mayor in the 1992 elections was Eduardo Suplicy, who, in marked contrast with Erundina, came from an extremely wealthy family. He belonged to another faction within the PT and hardly mentioned her achievements in his electoral material. His defeat at the hands of the veteran right-winger and old ally of the military, Paulo Maluf, brought a return to old-style politics with a vengeance.

* * *

Another woman, Telma de Souza, was elected mayor of the port of Santos during the same 1988 elections that catapulted Erundina into office in São Paulo. A vivacious and charismatic woman in her early 40s, Telma was the daughter of a militant Santos docker. Just like Erundina, she benefited from the fact that elections in 1988 were still decided in a single round. Telma was elected with under a third of the votes and might well have lost, had there been a run-off.

Like Erundina, Telma had a difficult first year in office. Because the PT was weak in Santos, the head office provoked initial resentment among local people by sending in experienced administrators from other parts of the country, including Davi Capistrano, later elected as Telma's successor. The PT, which had not expected to win and had not prepared a detailed plan for government, announced a radical, if somewhat vague, programme. It said that it intended to 'invert priorities', giving pride of place to the periphery of the town, rather than the centre, and to poor people, rather than the rich. It had four priority areas: public transport, health, education and housing.

Serious conflicts soon arose. The private bus company, which had a virtual monopoly over bus transport in the town, refused to improve its services and the municipal administration began a long legal battle to expropriate it. Telma, a pyschotherapist whose cousin had died after electric shock treatment in a mental hospital, was horrified at the state of the local asylum. It was extremely overcrowded, housing 600 patients instead of the 200 for which it was built, and was clearly failing to provide anything like adequate treatment for many of its inmates. Men and women were left naked, sharing buckets for toilets. Many were over-sedated. Telma embarked on a personal crusade to open up the asylum and re-house many of the inmates in the community, beginning a long legal battle to take over the hospital. Four or five times medical staff sent in by the municipal authorities were evicted from the asylum by the police, carrying out court orders. The battle split public opinion in the town down the middle.

Telma eventually won both battles. She closed down the private bus company, replacing it with a municipal corporation that reduced fares and increased the frequency of the buses. Eventually, she also took over the mental asylum. Many of the patients were allowed back into the community, where they were treated at new mental health posts opened by the authorities. The patients began to paint and to learn to play musical instruments. They even began to run their own daily radio show, lasting one hour and still going on today, during which they act as disc jockeys and interview musicians. Despite some initial resistance from the community, the project proved a great success, earning international recognition. Telma sees it as her proudest achievement.

The PT's outstanding success in improving general health care was chiefly responsible for Telma's growing support among the people of Santos. The administration took seriously the requirement in the 1988 constitution that good health care should be freely available to everyone, whether or not they had paid national health contributions. The public health system was decentralised and health centres known as *policlínicas* were set up all over the city. These centres do not give emergency care, but provide all the routine health care services, including pre-natal check-ups and vaccinations for children. Santos has the highest rate of AIDS infection in Brazil, probably because thousands of sailors visit it each year, and all the *policlínicas* have a special section providing counselling and medical care for HIV-infected and AIDS patients and their families. The *policlínicas* are the population's first port-of-call, with doctors referring more serious cases on to the hospitals. The scheme has been an undoubted success and each month delegations from other municipal administrations, controlled by a range of different political parties, visit Santos to study its health system.

The administration made an impact in other areas. As the nearest seaside town to São Paulo, Santos had once been a popular holiday resort, but over the previous decade the number of holiday-makers had fallen off heavily due to the high level of pollution on the beaches. Experts attributed most of the pollution to the river, which carried effluents and sewage from the city of São Paulo down to Santos. It seemed that little could be done, short of a multi-billion dollar anti-pollution programme in São Paulo.

The PT administration decided to have another look at the problem. Its study challenged the conventional wisdom, concluding that most of the effluents from São Paulo were swept far out to sea, and the pollution on the beaches came from the town's own sewage, discharged illegally into the canals that cut across the town. The solution was remarkably simple; close the lock gates across the canals just before they reached the beaches and channel their waters into the town's sewage treatment plant. The proposal was ridiculed, especially by São Paulo state technicians, as typical *petista* nonsense.

Eventually, however, the state water company agreed to test the scheme, particularly as it required only minimal investment. Overnight, pollution dropped and within a year the beaches were clean. Tourism is now booming, bringing new money into the town. Telma believes that the most important achievement in cleaning up the beaches was not in finding a technical solution to a technical problem. 'We had to fight to get our proposal taken seriously,' she says. 'We had to mobilise the population through the 16 popular councils that we set up – *that* was the most important part. It helped people to regain their feeling of citizenship, their feeling of empowerment. They became proud once again of living in Santos. That's what a PT administration is all about.'

The municipal administration has been careful over how it has incorporated popular participation into the daily administration of the town. Some, but not all, of the popular councils have been given deliberative powers. Those not believed to be sufficiently representative have remained advisory. The administration has held a large number of municipal conferences, covering areas such as health, education and the environment, to which mass-based organisations send delegates, who in turn elect the popular councils. To increase public understanding of the administration's finances and to gauge the priorities of the mass-based organisations, the PT also holds an annual Municipal Budget Congress. According to Davi Capistrano, 'these conferences are cumbersome and time-consuming, but they are the best way we have yet found of strengthening participatory democracy.'

The authority of the municipal administration was challenged in 1991 by President Fernando Collor de Mello when he announced, without prior consultation, the privatisation of the port of Santos. Overnight about 5,300 dockers were to be sacked. Immediately the powerful dockers' union went on strike and, despite intimidation from the federal government, the municipal administration organised a highly effective 24-hour sympathy strike in Santos. Collor was forced to back down and, though privatisation is still going ahead, it now involves far greater consultation with the workforce.

Telma also paid a great deal of attention to the history and culture of Santos. She opened museums, restored a crumbling statue of an old lion, much loved by the local inhabitants, and planted flower beds along the promenade. 'Perhaps it's a woman's way of doing politics,' she says. 'We women have learnt how to be tough. You should have seen me during the strike against Collor! Men have now got to learn to be more sensitive and understanding, to spend time with their children, to become good parents. It's not the kind of message that the PT likes to hear, but for me it's all-important.'

By the end of Telma's four-year term, 84 per cent of the population considered her administration to be 'good' or 'excellent'. Not surprisingly, Davi Capistrano, who had been health secretary in Telma's administration, was elected mayor in 1992, with a comfortable majority of 30,000 votes.

Davi does not have Telma's warm, captivating personality, which has made her so widely loved in Santos, and she is privately critical of his failure to care for the small, personal details that she finds so important. But he is a competent administrator and a committed *petista*. He is carrying on with the general lines of her administration, paying more attention to housing, which he believes was somewhat neglected under Telma. He is particularly proud of a project for resettling on firm ground shanty-town dwellers currently living in shacks mounted on poles to protect them from chronic floods.

When asked to name his most serious problem, he replies, 'Our very success.' Because the public services provided by the Santos administration are far better than those elsewhere in the region, people are pouring in to use its health centres, schools and hospitals. Homeless people move to Santos from other towns to squat illegally on private land so that they can benefit from the administration's housing programme for homeless families. All this, says Davi, is putting enormous pressure on the administration's finances.

* * *

In the same elections in 1988, the PT candidate was elected mayor of Porto Alegre, the capital of the southernmost state of Brazil, Rio Grande do Sul. With a population of 1.3 million inhabitants, Porto Alegre has its own peculiarities. Its citizens are much better-off than the average Brazilian, with an average income of around US$4,000, twice the national average. The city has a low illiteracy rate of just 8.7 per cent and has long been a centre of opposition among both trade unionists and the middle class. The Landless Peasant Movement was born in Porto Alegre, which was also the first city to elect PT federal deputies.

Nevertheless, the PT was not expecting its candidate, Olívio Dutra, to win in 1988. Two other large parties were fielding strong candidates and it was widely assumed that one of them would win. Just as in the case of Telma de Souza in Santos, Olívio Dutra's life story helps explain why he was able to pull off the victory (see page 44).

Just as in the other cities under PT administration, Olívio Dutra had a difficult first year. His main area of conflict concerned public transport. Dutra wanted the municipal council to take over the private bus companies, but he faced enormous resistance. Eventually, a compromise was worked out in which the private companies retained their fleets of buses, but agreed both to improve their service and to have their buses and their accounts more regularly inspected by the municipal authorities.

As in Santos, the PT's breakthrough came with its successful social policies. During Dutra's four-year term of office, the number of houses on a mains sewerage system increased six-fold, and there were huge improvements in the educational system. By the end of his term in office, 60 per cent of the population considered his administration 'good' or 'excellent'. In the 1992 elections, Dutra's vice-mayor, Tarso Genro, one of the party's liveliest thinkers, won easily in the first round, running under the slogan 'Porto Alegre wants more'.

Porto Alegre's political innovation has been its success in introducing popular councils with full deliberative powers. The experiment was started by Dutra and further developed by Tarso Genro. Today a series of neighbourhood councils elect councillors onto a Participatory Budget Council which has full control over one quarter of the administration's budget. It is widely considered the PT's most successful example of direct democracy, and left-wing political culture seems to be winning over the population; Rio Grande do Sul was the only state where Lula beat Fernando Henrique Cardoso in the 1994 presidential election.

In the 1992 elections the PT won in three other state capitals apart from Porto Alegre: Belo Horizonte, Goiânia and Rio Branco, as well as in fifty other mainly medium-sized towns. PT activists' growing experience in local government is both giving them a chance to put into practice some of their ideas and changing the way they see the world, as these tales show:

Ribeirao Preto

In 1980 a group of medical students in Ribeirao Preto, a prosperous town in the interior of the state of São Paulo, founded a PT nucleus. Fifteen years later these students have put on weight, had children and opened medical practices. Many, however, have remained in the PT. One is 33-year old Antônio Palocci Filho. During this time he has been a local councillor, a state deputy and since 1992, the town's mayor. Once a member of a Trotskyist tendency within the PT, today he holds more moderate views. He spends his days grappling with local government accounts, responding to wage demands from the administration's employees, and keeping up with technological innovations, because the council runs (at a profit) the local telephone exchange. 'Ten years ago I would never have imagined that I could end up here,' says Palocci. 'I was involved in student politics to combat the military dictatorship. Running the local council was the last thing I thought I would be doing.'

Londrina

In 1983 the lecturer, Lygia Pupatto, was giving botany lessons in the state University of Londrina in the coffee-growing state of Paraná. Concerned about the low level of wages earned by university teachers, she got involved in the local union and joined the PT. In 1992, when the PT won the election for mayor of Londrina, Lygia became a local councillor. She works harder than ever, without enough time to spend with her two daughters, but says she is benefiting a great deal from the experience, 'When I joined the PT, we spoke a lot about the conflict between labour and capital,' she says. 'Now we're discovering that there can be labour-labour conflicts. Sometimes we have to make hard choices, deciding, for instance, whether to pay better wages to our employees or invest money on sewerage for the shanty towns on the outskirts of the city.'

* * *

In the 1994 elections in October 1994, two PT candidates won for the first time the election for state governor: Victor Buaiz in the state of Espírito Santo and Cristovam Buarque in the Federal District of Brasília. The backgrounds of the two men, and the kind of government they might be expected to head, are very different:

Vitor Buaiz

Buaiz, governor of the state of Espírito Santo, is unrepentently middle class. A qualified doctor, he got involved in politics through the trade union of medical doctors. 'I've known Lula for over 15 years, since before the PT was founded, through our union activity,' he says. 'We're good friends, but we're completely different. I was elected federal deputy and then mayor of Vitória (capital of Espírito Santo) with the support of the middle and upper classes.'

Buaiz was a successful mayor, greatly improving public services, particularly the health service (as might be expected). The experience profoundly marked his political outlook, he says, 'The PT has a doctorate in criticising, in radicalising, in opposing, in drawing up projects and proposals. But it still has to learn how to govern, to respond to the immediate needs of the whole of the population.' He also believes that the PT must learn how to make electoral alliances, explaining, 'I was elected mayor with the support of the social democrats.'

Buaiz gained a comfortable victory in the 1994 elections for state governor, even though Lula lost the election for president in the state. Buaiz comments, 'Surveys show that sixty per cent of the people in Espírito Santo who voted for Fernando Henrique for president, voted for Buaiz for governor. People still vote for individuals, not parties.' Perhaps because of this, Buaiz called on people to vote for Lula, but failed to criticise Fernardo Henrique during his free time on television during the electoral campaign. Buaiz reacts evasively to critics from within the PT, 'My time on television is so short, that I'm not going to waste it attacking anyone.'

The governor has dared to raise one of the PT's taboo subjects; Lula's suitability as the party's presidential candidate. 'Market surveys show that sixty per cent of people in Espírito Santo with university degrees vote for me. People like that don't vote for Lula. Just out of pure prejudice, society – and many of my voters – can't accept a president who was once a metalworker. Someone like Erundina wouldn't face Lula's problems. She has the right profile. She is charismatic, comes from the social movements, is a north-easterner, was mayor of the largest city in Brazil. She has most of what Lula has and a little more, through the fact that she was a social worker. She wouldn't face the prejudice that Lula does.'

Much of what the governor proclaims is heresy for many *petistas*. What redeems Buaiz in their eyes is his undoubted commitment to social reform. 'There is no point in the state getting rich, if the people remain poor, going hungry,' he announced on taking office. He is giving priority to social services and small farmers and to imposing far greater environmental controls over large economic groups, like the paper and pulp manufacturer

Aracruz Celulose, the mining company *Companhia Vale do Rio Doce*, and the steel manufacturer *Companhia Siderúrgica de Tubarão*.

Cristovam Buarque

Throughout his professional life 50-year old Cristovam Buarque, governor of the Federal District of Brasília, has been something of a maverick. A lecturer in economics, he has done pioneering work in many controversial fields. He was one of the first to demand that conventional economic indicators, like gross domestic product (GDP), take into account the environmental and social damage that economic growth can cause. He formulated the concept of 'social apartheid', showing how the rift between the haves and have-nots was rapidly expanding in Brazilian society. It was a concept that was adopted enthusiastically by those drawing up the PT's political manifesto in 1993.

Cristovam spent nine years in exile in the 1970s, driven out by the military dictatorship. He earned a doctorate in economics at the Sorbonne, returning to Brazil in 1979 to lecture at Brasília University, where, in the mid-1980s, he was elected chancellor. Only when his term was over, in 1989, did he join the PT, where his creativity was soon recognised and he became part of Lula's shadow cabinet during the Collor administration.

When he was selected as the PT's candidate for governor in Brasília, he was an outsider, with opinion polls suggesting that he would obtain less than ten per cent of the vote. His remarkable victory was partly luck, in that voters were growing tired of the control exercised over the federal capital by one of the established parties, and partly political verve, particularly Cristovam's excellent performance in televised debates.

As ever, Cristovam did not hesitate to be controversial during the campaign. One of his most widely publicised proposals was to make a monthly payment, equal to one minimum wage, to every poor family that had been living in the city for at least five years and had at least one child attending school. According to Cristovam's calculations, this innovatory proposal would cost less than one per cent of the Federal District budget. He hopes that it will lead to a surge in the number of children from poor families who are regularly attending school, which has long been one of his main concerns.

Cristovam's victory came as a great surprise, not least to himself. He says that he is not a professional politician and will be returning to the university once his term is over.

* * *

Such victories are giving the PT ample opportunity to strengthen direct democracy and to experiment with new forms of popular participation.

Encouragingly, the PT tends to perform better in elections in regions of the country that have already been under its control, a phenomenon which in the aftermath of Lula's defeat in 1994, led many *petistas* to conclude that, rather than attacking the federal government and denouncing the evils of social apartheid, the PT in 1994 would have been better advised to concentrate on publicising its undoubted achievements in local government.

7

Conclusion

The story of the Brazilian Workers' Party and its leader, Luís Inácio da Silva, has a significance that goes far beyond Brazil. Its attempt to create effective citizenship attacks the central problem faced by a growing number of the 'excluded' in countries around the globe, who face the uncertainties of a world dominated by the disorder of a rampant liberal capitalism. The PT's fate is a litmus test for the chances of reviving the socialist dream of a democratic, egalitarian society anywhere.

During its remarkable growth over the last 15 years, the PT has had to address universal issues, such as how to forge democratic but effective links with grassroots movements and how to bring its ethics of idealism and self-denial into the dirty world of politics. It has also grappled with that classic conundrum for the Left; why do the poorest and most exploited groups in society often refuse to elect into government people like themselves, choosing, instead, one of their oppressors? While still exhibiting many of the traits of classical left-wing movements, the PT has forged a new way of relating to grassroots social movements, and has developed an open political culture that brings together radicalism and tolerance, lofty intellectual debate and the unscholarly demands of landless peasant activists.

The 1994 elections were a great disappointment to most *petistas*, for they failed to install Lula in the presidency, even though victory had seemed almost inevitable at the beginning of the year. But by strengthening the PT's presence in Congress, the elections highlighted the way in which the party is different. In a Congress dominated by landowners and bankers, almost all of the PT's representatives are workers, trade union leaders, teachers, activists from mass-based movements or renowned intellectuals. In the Senate, where highly conservative male politicians have always reigned supreme, the PT now has five seats, including two held by women – the black shanty-town leader, Benedita da Silva, and the daughter of an Amazonian rubber-tapper, Marina da Silva.

The greatest irony of Lula's electoral defeat was that it carried into the presidency Fernando Henrique Cardoso, a former Marxist and prominent opponent of the military regime that ruled Brazil from 1964 to 1985. Cardoso's main intellectual influence in his formative years was Karl Marx.

Without the threat of a Lula victory, Cardoso would not have gained the support of a wide coalition of political forces, ranging from the centre to the extreme right.

The new alliance around Cardoso represents an important development. For the first time ever, the leading conservative forces in Brazil have agreed to relinquish direct political control in favour of supporting, from a subordinate position, a committed democrat. It is the first substantial concession made by Brazil's ruling élite for more than half a century, and it can in some ways be seen as a victory for democracy. Cardoso formulated the influential theory of dependency, which held that the cause of Latin America's woes lay largely with its role in the international economy and its relationship with the colonial powers.

Today Cardoso sees things very differently. In an article published simultaneously in the United States and Europe just before the Americas Summit in Miami in December 1994, Cardoso wrote, 'Today most sociologists and political scientists, especially in developing countries, see integration and participation in the world market as the solution to their problems, not the cause of their difficulties. Above all, the "zero sum game", in which one country's gain is another's loss, has lost credence. Today one no longer talks winners and losers, but of balancing forces, based on fair negotiations between nation states.' As a result, Cardoso has the support of the international financial market, which sees him as the right man to take up and complete the market-oriented, neoliberal reforms begun by President Fernando Collor de Mello, before he was forced out of office on corruption charges.

There will, however, be a Brazilian version of the neoliberal model. Cardoso believes that for a country as large and as important as Brazil there is considerable room for manoeuvre, and that Brazil will not be forced to implement neoliberalism in its crudest and most painful form. He will try to cushion the restructuring with a large number of social initiatives that would not be undertaken by a straightforwardly conservative government. When taking office, Cardoso gave great emphasis to this part of programme, proclaiming, 'This is the great challenge that faces Brazil at the end of the 20th Century – social justice.' He will apparently model his measures on the 'Solidarity' programme carried out by President Carlos Salinas de Gortari in Mexico, which, at least until the Zapatista rebellion in early 1994, seemed to have had considerable success in defusing social unrest. Such programmes form part of the old tradition of populist politics. They are devised not to change the system but to sustain it by easing its tensions. They are intended to erode support for the organised Left by creating an alternative, clientelistic channel for government action at local level.

If successful, a neoliberal programme with substantial compensatory social policies would represent an enormous theoretical and practical challenge to the PT, all the more so because Cardoso's administration may well mark the end of one economic cycle and the beginning of a new and lasting one, under the aegis of neoliberalism. A new cycle of Brazilian development would have an enormous impact throughout Latin America. The realisation that the PT had failed to come to power at a crucial turning point in Brazilian history has turned the party's internal post-electoral discussion into a debate on its failure to win the big prize, rather than a celebration of its continued electoral growth, winning two state governorships for the first time.

* * *

In public, the PT often appears confused over its policies, partly because of its constant internal debates over strategy. One example is its approach to the state. Brazil is at the end of a fifty-year-long economic cycle, based on state intervention in the economy to bring about rapid industrialisation, a process known as import substitution. State companies, greatly favoured during the years of military government, are hotbeds of corruption and political patronage. Their inefficiency has meant that, until the recent reductions in trade barriers, consumers were forced to pay absurdly high prices for essential modern products, such as computers and telephone lines, manufactured under the aegis of the state. As a result, most Brazilians are hostile to the state and receptive to the simple message from right-wing parties that state companies must be privatised.

In contrast, the PT recommends a complex scheme for the 'democratisation of state companies', indeed, for the 'democratisation of the whole state', without really explaining what it means. What the PT is saying is that to set limits on the multinational companies, Brazil needs a strong and efficient state that is responsive to the needs and wishes of the people it is protecting, and that the best way of achieving this is to open up the state so that the people who are employed by it, and the people who receive its services, have a far greater say in the way it is managed. It is an important proposal, but it is an abstract idea that cannot be readily grasped by most people.

In the same way Lula's somewhat naive commitment to giving priority to domestic industry – 'I would rather pay a dollar and a half for a Brazilian T-shirt than a dollar for one imported from Taiwan', he said repeatedly on his campaign trail – sounds outdated to many Brazilians who increasingly see themselves as global consumers. Nor does it reflect the position of many economists within the PT, who see the growing integration of the world economy as inevitable. The challenge, they say, is to combine it with a strong state sector and radical measures to redistribute income.

The PT tends to couch its proposals in terms that seem to many not just quaintly old-fashioned, but dangerously out of touch with the modern world. Along with trade unionists, some traditional left-wing activists helped found the party and they have always had a key influence in formulating the concepts used by the party. As a result, the party tends to use an outdated Leninist language, talking of 'taking over the state' and 'building popular power', which tends to frighten off today's voters.

Another area where the party needs to define its views more clearly is the whole issue of socialism, which is provoking a lively debate within the party. For a long while the party did not need to define precisely what kind of socialism it sought. Socialism was a vague reference to something that would be developed in the distant future. While being strongly anti-Stalinist, many PT members looked with sympathy at the efforts to construct socialism in eastern Europe and with even more friendliness at the Cuban experiment. This was a natural result of the Cold War, which made progressives choose between capitalism, which had a particularly savage character in Latin America, and 'actually existing' socialism. The party was just beginning to define what it meant by socialism when suddenly it was all over, with the collapse of the Berlin Wall.

Since then, the discussion has moved on. Did the collapse of the Berlin Wall liberate the Latin American Left from a burden causing it nothing but trouble, as Lula claims, echoing the Mexican thinker, Jorge Castañeda? If so, how is socialism to be defined in the modern world? Or are today's challenges so different that socialism has become an idea whose time has passed, as some members of the PT believe? And, in this case, what is to replace the socialist utopia? Is the Left destined to be no more than a reformist movement in the post-cold-war world? Can socialism really coexist with democracy, as the PT has always claimed, or is socialism intrinsically authoritarian?

Some former socialists are rejecting not only socialism, but also post-war social democracy, in that they no longer believe in an important role for the state. In Brazil this group is strong outside the PT, and includes many members of President Fernando Henrique Cardoso's Social Democratic Party who, strictly speaking, should no longer be called social democrats but liberal democrats. But there is a group within the PT, including an influential activist, Tarso Genro, mayor of Porto Alegre, which defends a radical version of these views. Tarso Genro argues that the PT has failed to grasp the scale of the socialist collapse and is trying to cover the wounds of socialism with a social-democratic sticking plaster which, he says, is as outdated as classic socialism. Defining his ideas as a 'humanist-socialist project', he is calling for a whole new approach compatible with the dynamics of today's world.

The PT has a further problem, not faced by the other political parties, in its attempt to put its message across to the population. Many of its proposals run counter to the dominant values of modern life, which are overwhelmingly disseminated by the mass media. A massive media bombardment, promoting self-interest, individualist values, faith in the market as a solution for all economic problems, and the prevailing belief that the search for personal happiness is the only worthwhile goal in life, also attempts to portray the PT vision as hopelessly outdated and idealistic.

However, it is possible to overcome such barriers. Many Brazilians do not reject radicalism in itself; what they distrust are inconsistency and confusion. Cristovam Buarque, an innovative PT economist and the first person to develop the concept of social apartheid, has shown that it is possible to win popular support for radical proposals. Presenting a coherent and well-argued manifesto that demanded that every poor family should be guaranteed a minimum income and that radical measures should be taken to reduce urban pollution, he won the 1994 election for the governorship of the Federal District of Brasília, defeating a powerful populist opponent and his well-oiled political machine.

Another issue thrown up by Lula's 1994 electoral defeat is how the PT, a mass party, is to promote itself in the age of electronic politics. Lula is a powerful public speaker, with a rare ability to communicate with ordinary Brazilians. He comes across best at mass rallies, where he is far more effective than Fernando Henrique Cardoso, as any journalist who has followed them both on the campaign trail will vouch. Yet, as elsewhere in the world, mass rallies are losing importance in Brazil. The 1994 campaign was dominated by television, where, under the guidance of the US public relations company that had advised Bill Clinton, Cardoso was marketed with slick efficiency. In what amounted to little more than an intelligent adaptation of Clinton's TV commercials, Cardoso was pictured sitting at his desk, answering the telephone, talking to foreign dignitaries. He exuded authority, confidence and modest affluence.

In contrast Lula, whose class origin is stamped on his face, often looked uncomfortable and awkward, particularly in a suit, shirt and tie. He came across as earnest and well-meaning, but not a statesman. It was an impression exacerbated by the strict (and unfair) electoral regulations that banned the broadcast of video footage of mass rallies during the period of free electoral advertising. Some PT members believe that the party must simply accept that elections are now won or lost on TV. Lula, with his proletarian image, may not be the party's most effective candidate, they say. Others argue that the PT has always bucked the trend and that it can still set its own agenda, hold its mass rallies, mobilise its supporters and win the race, proving that the age of mass party politics is not over.

The key to success in this strategy is the party maintaining strong and binding links with its grassroots, and it is this, far more than the 1994 electoral defeat, that is most worrying some veteran activists. They say that, seduced by the electoral process, many *petistas* are placing far too much importance on winning elections and are beginning to lose the ethical purity that distinguished them from supporters of other political parties. During the 1994 campaign, several PT candidates accepted substantial contributions from large private companies, including building contractors previously involved in political corruption. Although the contributions were made in strict adherence to the law, this has shaken the party's rank-and-file more than any ideological conflict.

Florestan Fernandes, a renowned social scientist and one of the founding members of the PT, pointed out that the party would not have needed to accept the money if it had placed more emphasis on raising people's political awareness, rather than just winning seats in Congress. Before he demonstrated the allure of power by joining the Cardoso government, Francisco Weffort was even more critical of the way in which the tantalising prospect of presidential victory had cast a spell over the party. In an interview with the party's most important internal publication, he warned, 'We were the party that invented this idea that the party must have a cultural life, a permanent social life, outside the electoral process. Yet immediately after the 1989 elections, we started putting stickers on our cars saying "Happy 1994". A party that changes its mind in this way is doomed to failure.' Yet, he says, this is not how it needs to be, 'The PT's trajectory has not been one of defeat. Up to now – and probably into the future – our story has been one of victory and of constant growth. Only the PT can defeat the PT.'

Despite its inconsistencies and inner turbulence, the PT is still growing rapidly. Over the next few years it will broaden its administrative skills and experience, now that it also runs state governments. Faced with the challenge of the Cardoso government, it will also have to work out more clearly the alternative it offers to his version of neoliberalism with a human face. Over 17 million people cast their vote for Lula in the first round of the 1994 presidential election, compared with 12 million in the first round of the 1989 election. In the eyes of millions more Brazilians every year, the PT represents their best hope for a better world.

8

Lula in Conversation

In December 1994 one of the authors, Bernardo Kucinski, interviewed Lula in his office in the PT headquarters in São Paulo. Lula was good-humoured and lively. Telephone calls came in continuously from all over Brazil. Despite the internal debate about Lula's future in the wake of his second presidential defeat, he still seemed to be at the very centre of party affairs.

On Socialism

BK: Social democrats all over the world are saying that socialism is dead, that the Left must give up the socialist utopia if it wants to have a real chance of being elected to power. A few *petistas*, such as José Genoíno, a one-time Maoist guerrilla, seem to accept this view. Others are sticking more firmly than ever to socialism. What do you think?

Lula: There are two opposing views in the Workers' Party. One, the more orthodox view, is that we should go on holding the same opinions as before as if nothing had happened at all in the world, and that we should even use the former socialist countries as models. The other view is simply that socialism is dead. Personally, I never supported what was called 'real socialism', that is, the socialism that existed in eastern Europe until 1990, so I have no reason now to wring my hands and say I got it wrong. In fact, I feel more socialist all the time. If you can accept the fact that 80 per cent of our wealth is concentrated in the hands of only 20 per cent of the population, while the other 80 per cent of Brazilians get only 20 per cent of the wealth, then you can support the capitalist system of production. But I don't accept it. People keep talking about the virtues of the capitalist system in Denmark, Germany, Switzerland, but they don't mention Brazil, India, Peru, Bolivia, Africa.

We must seek a model of society in which there is a fairer distribution of wealth. You don't even need to call it a socialist project; call it a Christian project, or an ethical project. Instead of socialism, call it the defence of human rights, or the defence of citizenship. For me, the label is unimportant;

what matters is the content. In my view, the best way to increase people's awareness is not going into the street waving the banner of socialism, but by talking about the Constitution, the Children's Charter, or the Universal Charter of Human Rights, and asking people to fight for it. You get better results that way than with a general speech about the virtues of socialism.

BK: Some critics within the PT say the party should concentrate on educating workers and raising their awareness, instead of putting so much energy into winning seats in Congress or gaining control of local administrations. How do you react to this criticism?

Lula: It's illogical. Only by being elected to office can we have some influence over our political institutions, can we show that we are different – unless the idea is to raise mass awareness not in order to win elections, but to seize power. In that case we have a serious disagreement, because I think that the PT must seize power through democratic means. I've seen what a difference it makes for a town to have a PT administration. And the party immediately starts growing. It has a public image, takes part in the main political debates. This is good. We must never lose our links with the social movements, but it is extremely important to elect representatives at all levels, and for them to defend the interests of ordinary people.

BK: I remember how, at the height of the 1994 campaign, a group of Cuban boatpeople landed on the Brazilian coast, in the state of Bahia. One of them gave an interview on television in which he described how his son had fallen into the sea during a storm and been eaten by a shark. The television station didn't use the incident to attack socialism, but it struck me all the same how difficult it was for the PT to win people over, particularly the middle classes and the young, at a time when the image of Cuba in the media is so negative, when it seems that the Cuban revolution has finally been defeated. Do you think this was relevant to your defeat in 1994?

Lula: Socialism was not the issue in the 1994 campaign; there was no ideological debate. The decisive issue was the new stable currency, the *Real*. The propaganda around the Cuban boat people makes me wonder what would happen if Brazil's shore was only 90 miles away from Miami, of how many thousands of Brazilians would try to reach the US. What people try to do is leave a place of extreme poverty and go to one of plenty. That is why the north-easterners trekked 2,000kms to the south, as my parents did. Too much is made of the fact that the boatpeople are Cuban. In fact, though the Soviet Union doesn't exist any more, anti-communism hasn't ended. What is happening in Cuba happens everywhere where there

Tony Samphier

is shortage. You won't see a German, or an Englishman, leaving their rich Europe to come and settle in miserable Brazil today.

BK: The Latin American Left looks to the PT as its benchmark. How do you see the region's Left at a time when neoliberalism still seems to be dominant?

Lula: The Left is advancing in Latin America. There was an extraordinary advance in Uruguay in the recent elections. In Argentina the left opposition is growing. In Venezuela the social democrats won, but the Left is playing an increasingly important role. In Mexico, new forms of opposition are emerging. These are big steps forward for the Left. We must remember that until 1990 the Latin American Left didn't even meet to talk to each other. Today we are working out common policies; we have learned to accept our differences. The PT is playing a decisive role in this process, if only because it is the largest left-wing party in Latin America.

On the 1994 campaign

BK: The common bond linking many militants in the PT is that they want morality in politics. During the last electoral campaign, when your victory seemed inevitable, some building contractors – who had been exposed a year earlier by the PT itself as the main agents of political corruption – contributed to the party's campaign funds. Some *petistas* have been highly critical of this, and of the party's decision to make alliances in the second round of the election with political parties it fought in the first round. How do you see these moral issues?

Lula: We mustn't confuse ethics with political stupidity. First of all, political alliances are made between parties that are different. People with the same views belong to the same party; they do not need to make alliances. Secondly, getting money from this kind of donor will only mean a loss in ethics if the party changes the way it behaves. Not only party militants, but many other people, don't understand this. If a company donates US$10,000 – or US$50,000 – to the PT, and then later this same company is accused of some wrongdoing and the PT backs away from demanding a full investigation, then and only then will the party be betraying its ethics. Another point: the PT cannot pay for a presidential campaign just by selling badges. It is a question of choice: either the rank-and-file finds alternative means of financing a national campaign, or it has to accept the law which lets companies donate money to political parties. But I'm not critical of militants who are angry about this. I know that it's a delicate issue that the party has to discuss carefully. It is part of our culture; the party leadership has to explain all its actions.

BK: Do you think that the PT's failure to present a clear idea of the political model it wanted was a serious liability? Did voters sense a lack of ideological clarity? Eduardo Suplicy, the PT senator who first proposed the creation of a minimum family income, claims that Cristovam Buarque won in Brasília because he included such a proposal high on his agenda. Do you think your campaign should have been more, not less, radical?

Lula: I think that the proposal for a minimum income is all right from a philosophical point of view, but weak from a practical point of view. I know that the scheme has been successfully implemented in some European countries, but the situation in Brazil is completely different. In a European country you might have five million or so people out of work and another fifty million people or so employed and earning reasonably well. In Brazil it is the other way round. I don't share the view that the unemployed in Brazil should be given left-overs. What they need is the opportunity to work and earn a decent wage.

BK: The media in Brazil, and in the whole of Latin America, is strongly concentrated in the hands of the ruling classes. Shouldn't the Left pay more attention to democratising the media as a way of guaranteeing fairer political debate?

Lula: I'm convinced that we will not get real democracy in Brazil until we have made the media more democratic. We must put an end to the ideological bias in the media. The Rícupero affair (see page 70) was, in its way, more serious than the Watergate affair in the USA. But while Watergate led to the downfall of Nixon, Rícupero was made an ambassador. If you go into the interior of the country, the situation is even worse. There, they are obliged by law to allow a left-wing candidate to speak on the radio for half an hour in the run-up to the election, but then they spend the rest of the year supporting the Right. The only way of changing the situation is by changing the way in which radio concessions are granted. Congress has an extremely important role here. It is not even a question of the level of education. Italy is an educated country, but Berlusconi won the election in three months because he owned a TV station. He could speak on television for a quarter of an hour each day while his opponents were only given two minutes.

On the PT's record in local government

BK: How important are municipal administrations, run by the party, in building the party? After some failures, the PT seems today to be doing well in a more consistent way, and has had some outstanding successes. The PT seems to have set a high standard for what it expects from a local administration. Do you think this could be the way to end the prejudice that workers are unable to govern themselves?

Lula: We have succeeded far more than we have failed. We have had some very rewarding experiences in local government. Look at Diadema, which was once just a huge shanty town and has become a beautiful town, which people feel proud to live in. It has the best public health system in the region. All its streets are paved and lit. Or take the case of Santos, where Telma de Souza ran a good administration. Porto Alegre and Vitória have both been total successes. Itabuna, in the state of Bahia, Cosmópolis, Angra dos Reis, all of them have been very successful. In São Paulo, Luiza Erundina did a good job, but she failed politically. There was a time when we, the PT, didn't believe in publicising our achievements, but we were wrong. In a huge place like São Paulo, if you do something good in the north of the city, people living in the south of it are unlikely to hear about it. I believe that we must publicise our successes, because our enemies will certainly let everyone know about our failures.

BK: Why then, with the exception of Diadema, did the PT lose the 1992 local elections in the ABCD industrial belt, where the PT was born and which used to be its stronghold?

Lula: São Bernardo and Santo André are two examples where we made, not administrative, but political mistakes. Our mayors in these towns spent more than anyone else on improving social conditions, but we failed on two levels: First of all, we were wrong, once again, not to publicise our achievements; secondly, internal disputes in both cases played a key role in our defeat. There were such big internal, highly personalised rows, that even some PT militants refused to vote for the party. I have no doubt that we will win back both towns in the next municipal elections.

BK: Since Brazil has around 5,000 municipal governments, should the party have a special strategy for local elections?

Lula: I think that throughout the country we should select the main towns that we can win by ourselves and then give these towns priority in our campaigning. There are also other towns where we can win by leading a front of popular forces, and yet others where our support could be crucial in gaining victory for a candidate from another political force. In order to strengthen the party, we should concentrate our efforts on a set of about 300 or 400 leading municipal administrations.

BK: Do you agree with the common criticism that the PT does not have enough well-prepared cadres to run local governments?

Lula: The PT has plenty of cadres, both intellectuals and unionists. Some of our cadres don't have much administrative experience, because we refused to work with the military governments, but we have even been successful when we have nominated young and inexperienced cadres. And new cadres are always appearing, once we show that we are competent and that the party monitors the local administrations that it runs.

On Internal Democracy

BK: There has always been room in the PT for all kinds of views; there has never been such a thing as an official party doctrine. But disagreements over the question of socialism seem to be getting worse. Do you think that the party is in danger of splitting?

Lula: I don't think so. What we have are natural disagreements in a democratic party. During the entire 15 years of our existence, the Brazilian press has always talked about irreconcilable divisions within the PT, but it's never been true. It's been invented by a press that's not used to a democratic party, in which everything is discussed and debated, sometimes to an excessive extent. But when the discussions end and a decision is taken, everybody adheres to it. After 25 years of military rule, the Brazilian press is obsessed with the idea of consensus, or of the need for a *caudillo* (party boss) to run a political party and to tell everybody what to do. But we created the PT precisely to be different. Every time they invent an internal war within the PT, we come out of it stronger.

BK: Some observers say that there are fewer workers in the PT these days; that the party has become a bureaucracy. But the party now has more workers and union leaders in Congress than ever before. There are also more ordinary people, not just intellectuals, at the party's rallies. How do you see the evolution of the party's social base?

Lula: We've always had a lot of unionised workers as militants. That is where our strength has always been and still is. But today the party has opened up to all kinds of other people. I don't think that we can become top-heavy with bureaucrats for the simple reason that we are still very poor. We haven't the money to support a bureaucracy. I have less administrative support for my work than if I was mayor of a small town. But I think that we urgently need to change the way in which we organise participation in the party. That is why I am proposing a membership drive to inject new life into the party, particularly young people and the more oppressed, non-politicised sectors of society. We must also change our political culture; we must charge an annual subscription. At the moment, no one pays fees and we have to survive on the compulsory contributions from PT deputies. It's our 15th anniversary this year, and it's time for the party to renew itself.

BK: What do you think about the party being organised around tendencies, which leaves almost no role for independent militants?

Lula: That's true. Today, if you're not a member of a particular tendency, you have no way of participating. But this problem will not be solved by decree. It is a culture. The party is organised around political groups. You only stand a chance of being elected as a delegate to the party's conventions if you belong to a tendency. What we must do is to encourage many more people, ordinary people not linked to any tendency, to join the party. They can help to change the balance of forces within the party, for example by electing 100 delegates out of a convention of 400. They'll then start having an influence on the party's decisions. That's why we need a new membership drive.

On Civil Resistance

BK: What do you think of Brazilian democracy? Do you foresee a time when Brazilians will have to resort more often to civil resistance? Do you think that the PT has neglected the potential of civil resistance and given too much emphasis to formal democracy?

Lula: In fact, it was civil resistance that gave birth to the PT. We went on strike when it was forbidden to do so. We created the PT against the advice of most of the left. But I think that today, far from benefiting from the violence, the Left is a victim of it. Only workers, trade unionists, peasant leaders, are killed in land conflicts in the countryside. Rich people are hardly ever killed. The Left has learnt a lot about politics from the PT, but it still seems not to have realised that you can't make politics without the participation of the people. Not enough attention is paid to the whole issue of people's awareness. We need to talk about new forms of political action, new methods.

We need to ask ourselves if we are doing enough, if what we are doing is right. For instance, we can't just speak for the working classes, because, even though they are still very important, they don't have the same weight in national politics as they had ten years ago. Today there are thousands and thousands of small entrepreneurs, shopkeepers, taxi-drivers, people of all kinds who do not feel that the PT represents their interests. It is not enough any more to talk to the worker at the factory gate. When he goes into the factory, he is a worker, but when he leaves, he becomes a citizen. We must broaden our discourse to address his various interests, as a citizen, as a consumer, as a family man.

On Cardoso's Government

BK: What are your expectations of Fernando Henrique Cardoso's administration? Do you think he will fulfil his pre-election promise to create ten million jobs and carry out land reform? Or will he end up running a kind of improved conservative administration, become a prisoner of the forces that helped elect him? And if his administration carries out deep structural reforms, how much room will be left for the PT?

Lula: I have been extremely careful not to assume that Fernando Henrique's administration will be a fiasco. First of all, because he has a political party, with cadres and ambitions. I have been saying insistently to people who criticise Fernando Henrique by comparing him with former Presidents Collor or Sarney, or Carlos Andrés Pérez of Venezuela, that he is much more like Spain's Felipe González. First of all, because he took part in the struggle for democracy; secondly, because he is linked to important sectors of civil society, and thirdly, because, like Margaret Thatcher and like the PT, he has a long-term project. Had the PT won, we would have drawn up a 15-year plan. They are hoping to stay in power for ten years or more. This means they must win the next presidential elections, so they will need to carry out some structural reforms to respond to the population's social demands.

They will be under contradictory pressures and there will be many internal conflicts, but they stand a good chance of attracting support from the centrist ranks of the PMDB [the country's largest political party] and of building up a reasonable hegemony. I have been suggesting to the PT that, instead of just opposing Cardoso's government in a negative way, we should offer specific alternatives, making it clear all the time what we want.

BK: It seems somewhat extreme to compare Fernando Henrique with Thatcher, since she has become the main symbol of neoliberal structural reforms. Is that what you mean?

Lula: Thatcher stayed in power for 12 years. No one was as competent as she was in implementing neoliberalism. I think that Fernando Henrique is behaving in a very similar way. I don't think he will bother much about protecting trade unions or developing the role of the state so that it can satisfy people's social needs. I remember Thatcher's scornful attitude towards the British miners, and her policy of importing coal from Poland. She won the election saying that the unemployed were a minority and that she addressed the needs of the majority. That, in a way, is how Fernando Henrique's mind works.

On Lula and the PT's future

BK: You have lost the presidential election for the second consecutive time. How do you see your political future? What are your priorities today?

Lula: My strictly personal wish is to go to a beach with the family and rest, but my priorities are not set by me. They are the party's priorities and the Brazilian people's priorities. So I will go on travelling around the country, trying to increase political awareness, improving the way we are organised, because that is the only way in which the Left can reach power.

BK: Do you agree with Fernando Henrique's belief that the Left on its own can never be elected to power in Brazil?

Lula: I think that he is partly right. Maybe the Left can reach power by itself, but it will take a long time. It can only happen when there is a far greater level of political awareness in the country, and that could take 15 or 20 years. Actually, I would rather that we took more time, gaining power in a consolidated manner, than get elected at any price and then be unable to deliver the structural reforms the country needs. But I agree that it is difficult to go it alone.

BK: The party grew much less in the last election than was expected. In many states, for instance, party candidates for the governorship got less than ten per cent of the votes. The PT had hoped to double its representation in Congress to seventy seats, following the collapse of the conservatives and the centre, after they had been shown to be deeply involved in corruption. But the PT only won 54 seats, including five senators. Do you think the party is reaching a kind of natural limit for this kind of party in Brazil? Is it destined to be a minority party?

Lula: I think that we are still growing well. Even though we elected fewer federal deputies than we expected and failed to elect two senators whose election looked certain – Luiza Erundina in São Paulo and Virgílio Guimarães in Minas Gerais – the election of five senators was a big surprise, a very important victory. In the presidential election, we obtained many more votes – five million more – than in the first round in 1989. That was a qualitative leap. Elections in Brazil are rather complex. This was a combined election, for legislative bodies, state governors and the president. And this affected the voting; in many states where our candidate for governor did badly, we got fewer votes than hoped for the presidency; but where local candidates were strong and made good alliances, I won a lot of support. In Mato Grosso, a conservative state, I got 25 per cent of the vote. In Rio Grande do Sul I got more votes than Fernando Henrique Cardoso. In Pernambuco and Bahia I got 36 per cent, a lot more than in 1989.

But I do think that, after 15 years, it is time for the party to rethink its strategy, to address the country in a different manner. We must redirect our actions away from the organised towards the non-organised sectors of society. We don't want to turn people into electoral cannon-fodder, as the conservatives do, but to increase their political awareness.

BK: Do you think the party's rank and file is prepared for partnerships with other parties, as it is used to a political culture in which the PT sees itself as morally superior to other parties?

Lula: The rank and file will accept it, if we debate the issue openly. We often act as if we shouldn't mix with other parties, as if we are superior, but this is wrong. We must stop thinking that we are the only ones who can do certain things. We must start realising that if we can't do something by ourselves, we must seek allies. Even within political parties that we consider our opponents, we can find people with a clean past who are prepared to support some of our policies. The rank and file will understand this, if we are able to explain it properly.

BK: Fernando Henrique, an opponent of the military regime and a former Marxist, got elected in a way because of the fear the Right had of you. Don't you feel this is an irony of fate?

Lula: In 1989 right-wing forces got Collor elected, saying that *Lula* (or Leonel Brizola) had to be blocked. In 1994 they managed to organise the widest political coalition ever formed in Brazil through fear of *Lula* becoming president. I feel good in a certain way, because I can see that the PT is being as beneficial to Brazil as social democracy was in Europe. The improvements obtained in European society, in particular in the post-war period, were mostly due to the fear of socialism, which forced capitalists to make concessions. Here in Brazil the government will have to improve living conditions for the mass of the people, for they know that, if they don't, the PT will go on expanding and the working classes will get more and more organised. Even if I fail to reach power, as long as they improve social conditions, that will still be an important achievement. Their problem is that I'm not a politician who ceases to exist the day after I lose an election, as happens with many conventional politicians. I will carry on travelling all over the country, organising people. And when 1998 arrives we will have an even stronger PT, and, if I'm not the candidate, there will certainly be a good PT candidate to run for president.

BK: The Catholic Church seems to be retreating from liberation theology into conventional religion. This was already clear during the 1994 campaign, when some PT leaders with a Catholic background failed to get re-elected. How do you see this?

Lula: People are always making the mistake of assuming that the PT is supported by the Catholic Church, but it has never supported us. What we have had is the backing of lay-workers and other Catholics active in the base Christian communities. The so-called 'progressive Church' has been losing ground, partly due to the conservative policies adopted by Pope John Paul II. He has reduced the power of certain progressively-minded bishops. Dom Paulo Evaristo Arns, archbishop of São Paulo, has had a large part of his archdiocese taken away from him. Dom Luciano Mendes de Almeida was moved from São Paulo to Mariana in the state of Minas Gerais. Other progressive bishops have retired and been replaced by conservatives. This has all meant that the progressive Church is far less active today than it was in 1989.

But we can't just blame the Pope for this – other factors have played a part. Political liberalisation has meant that people can take part in politics in other ways. The evangelical churches have grown rapidly, electing many right-wing politicians to Congress. Every time politics or economics fail to answer social needs, then people turn to the supernatural. This helps to explain why the evangelical churches, which are very conservative, have grown so rapidly. But in those areas where the base Christian communities are still strong, we are still getting good electoral results. In Paraná we even elected two priests as federal deputies.

BK: You seem to equate religion with the supernatural. But aren't you, yourself, a man of religion? Can't religion be different from this?

Lula: It can be different. While I think that people need to look after their spiritual lives, we mustn't forget the need too for political struggle as a way of changing society. I think that, besides its spiritual role, religion can help to open one's mind to social problems. But on many occasions religion has been used to manipulate people. I consider myself a man of religion, but I do not ignore social reality. I'm a man of religion who doesn't ask God for a wage rise, or for help in putting an end to famine.

Brazil in Brief

Population (1990)	150,368,000
Annual Growth rate (1990-95):	1.6 %
Urban (1990)	76.9 %
Area:	8,511,965 sq km (35 times the size of the United Kingdom)

Principal Cities:	Estimated Population (millions, mid 1989)
São Paulo	17.4
Rio de Janeiro	10.7
Belo Horizonte	3.6
Porto Alegre	3.1
Recife	2.5

People:

Main Language	Portuguese
Religion	Roman Catholic 80%; Protestant 16%
Origins:	European 56 %
	African 6 %
	Mixed 39 %

Brazil's indigenous inhabitants (Indians) number around 200,000

Social Indicators

Infant Mortality (1990-95)	56.5 per thousand live births
Life Expectancy (1990-95)	66.3 years
Illiteracy (1990)	18.9 %
Access to Safe Water (1988-91)	86 %

The Economy

Gross Domestic Product (1992) $US332,534 million

Trade (1992)   Exports $US40,378 million
                                  Imports $US25,792 million

Principal Exports (1992):

Metalurgical products   15.1%
Transport equipment & parts 10.4%
Soya beans   6.7%
Metal ores   6.3%

Main Trading Partners (1992):

Exports to: USA 19.7%; Argentina 8.5%;
                             Netherlands 6.5%; Japan 6.4%;
                             Germany 5.8%; United Kingdom 3.6%

Imports from: USA 24.0%; Germany 9.2%;
                             Argentina 8.2%; Japan 5.5%

Inflation: 1,294% (1994); 2,489% (1993)

Foreign Debt (1994) $151,500 million

Sources: UN Economic Commission on Latin America and the Caribbean
(ECLAC); Latin America Bureau; Inter-American Development Bank;
Economist Intelligence Unit; Brazilian government; UN Department of
International Economic and Social Affairs

Chronology

31 March 1964	Military coup overthrows President João Goulart
11 April 1964	After dozens of federal deputies have been arrested, Congress elects as president the coup leader, Marshall Humberto de Alencar Castello Branco.
1 June 1964	New law makes virtually all strikes illegal.
15 March 1967	Marshal Costa e Silva takes office as president.
12 October 1968	About 1,000 delegates at National Union of Students Congress are arrested.
3 December 1968	Government decrees Institutional Act 5, which dissolves Congress.
December 1968	Dissidents from the Brazilian Communist Party (PCB) take the name *Ação de Libertação Nacional* (ALN) and start armed struggle.
February 1969	Government declares Institutional Act 6, suspending the elections scheduled for later that year.
29 June 1968	The 2nd Army creates *Operação Bandeirantes* (OBAN), one of the main instruments of military repression.
31 August 1969	Taken ill with a heart attack, General Costa e Silva leaves the presidency. A military junta takes over, made up of the three heads of the armed forces.
4 September 1969	The US ambassador, Burke Elbrick, is kidnapped by the ALN and another urban guerrilla group, MR-8, and then freed in exchange for the release of 15 political prisoners and the publication in the press of a manifesto against the military dictatorship.
30 October 1969	General Emílio Garrastazu Médici becomes president.
12 April 1972	The army undertakes its first counter-insurgency operation against a guerrilla base created near the Araguaia river in the Amazon by a group within the Communist Party of Brazil (PC do B).
December 1972	Luís Inácio da Silva, known as 'Lula', takes over as director of the social welfare department of the Metalworkers' Union of São Bernardo and Diadema.
October 1973	The Movement against Price Increases (*Movimento Contra a Carestia*) organises its first mass demonstrations against the government's economic policy.
15 March 1974	General Ernesto Geisel takes over as president
October 1975	.Lula is elected president of the Metalworkers' Union of São Bernardo and Diadema.

17 January 1976	Manuel Fiel Filho, a young industrial worker, dies while held by DOI-CODI (the new name for OBAN).
March 1977	The Catholic Church's base Christian communities hold national assembly with 700 delegates.
2 May 1978	Metalworkers at the multinational company, Scania, in São Bernardo, start strike which rapidly spreads all over São Paulo state.
July 1978	For the first time Lula suggests the creation of a Workers' Party.
27 August 1978	The *Movimento Contra a Carestia* holds big demonstration in São Paulo and hands government a petition, signed by 1.3 million people, calling for measures to alleviate impact of economic crisis on poor.
10 October 1978	Institutional Acts are revoked.
14 March 1979	About 80,000 metal-workers from ABC towns around São Paulo go on strike.
15 March 1979	General João Baptista Figueiredo becomes president.
23 March 1979	Government closes down metalworkers' unions in ABC region.
27 March 1979	Lula accepts truce and metalworkers return to work.
June 1979	Strikes spread to rest of country.
10 February 1980	The Workers' Party is legally founded.
17 April 1980	Labour minister closes down Metalworkers' Unions of São Bernardo and Diadema, and Santo André.
19 April 1980	Lula and other union leaders are arrested.
1 May 1981	Two bombs go off during Mayday celebrations at Riocentro convention centre in Rio de Janeiro. Bombs are believed to have been planted by DOI-CODI, as part of a new right-wing terrorist offensive.
June 1981	Workers' Party has 200,000 members and can be registered in ten Brazilian states.
2 September 1981	The Supreme Military Tribunal quashes the prison sentences brought against Lula and other trade unionists.
27 September 1981	The Workers' Party holds its first official convention.
15 November 1982	Elections for state governors, state assemblies, senators, federal deputies, state deputies, mayors and local councillors. Workers' Party achieves 3.3 per cent of the vote, electing eight federal deputies.
27 November 1982	The Workers' Party holds the first demonstration in favour of direct elections for president, attracting 10,000 people.

25 January 1984	The Campaign for Direct Elections (*Diretas-Já*) is launched throughout the country.
January 1984	The Landless Peasant Movement (MST) is founded.
10 April 1984	A rally in favour of direct elections attracts over one million people in Rio de Janeiro.
25 April 1984	By small margin Congress votes against the Dante Oliveira amendment which would have re-established direct elections for president.
15 January 1985	The Electoral College selects Tancredo Neves as next president.
21 April 1985	Tancredo Neves dies without taking office. The vice-president, José Sarney, becomes president.
15 November 1985	The Workers' Party elects one mayor, in Fortaleza, in elections for mayors in state capitals.
28 February 1986	President Sarney announces *Cruzado* Plan.
11 April 1986	Five members of radical tendency within Workers' Party are arrested when robbing a bank in Salvador and are expelled from the party.
15 November 1986	Elections for governors, senators, and federal and state deputies. Workers' Party elects 16 deputies. Lula is the federal deputy with the highest number of votes (650,000).
5 October 1988	New Constitution comes into force.
15 November 1988	Elections for mayors and local councillors. Workers Party elects 29 mayors, winning three state capitals.
22 December 1988	Chico Mendes, the internationally-renowned rubber tapper, is assassinated.
15 November 1989	First round of presidential elections. Fernando Collor de Mello and Lula go through to second round.
11 December 1989	The businessman, Abílio Diniz, is kidnapped.
16 December 1989	Abílio Diniz is found and released. Evidence involving Workers' Party in kidnapping is fabricated.
17 December 1989	Collor de Mello wins the election, with 35 million votes, against 31 million going to Lula.
15 March 1990	Fernando Collor de Mello takes office
16 March 1990	Finance minister announces the Collor Plan, the harshest anti-inflation plan in Brazil's history.
2 July 1990	The São Paulo Forum, organised by the Workers' Party, is founded.
3 October 1990	Elections for governors, federal and state deputies, local councillors and one third of Congress. Workers' Party elects 35 deputies and its first senator.

8 February 1991	Dockers in Santos go on strike against government's plan to privatise port.
27 November 1991	First PT Congress
20 May 1992	The president's brother, Pedro Collor, gives interview to news magazine, *Veja*, which forces government to set up Congresssional enquiry into allegations of corruption made against the president's close aide, Paulo César Farias.
6-11 June 1992	Earth Summit held in Rio de Janeiro.
16 August 1992	Huge demonstration in São Paulo, with most participants wearing black armbands, calling for impeachment of President Collor for his involvement in corruption.
29 September 1992	By a large majority, Chamber of Deputies authorises Senate to judge President Collor for behaviour incompatible with high public office.
3 October 1992	First round of municipal elections.
15 November 1992	Second round of municipal elections. Workers' Party elects 55 mayors.
31 December 1992	President Collor resigns just hours before he would have been impeached by Senate. Senate strips him of his political rights for eight years.
1 January 1993	Itamar Franco takes over as interim president until end of Collor's term of office.
May 1993	Fernando Henrique Cardoso named as new Finance Minister in cabinet reshuffle
June 1993	PT National Meeting approves its campaign manifesto for 1994, stressing social apartheid, but failing to deal with inflation
May 1994	Lula has around 40 per cent support in opinion polls and seems set for victory in the presidential elections in October
1 July 1994	Government launches *Real* Plan.
3 October 1994	First round of elections for Congress, state governors, federal deputies, senators and state deputies. Fernando Henrique Cardoso wins with 34 million votes, against 17 million for Lula. The Workers' Party elects 49 federal deputies and 5 senators.
15 November 1994	Second round of elections. Workers' Party elects two state governors.
1 January 1995	Fernando Henrique Cardoso becomes president.

Source: Marta Harnecker *O Sonho Era Possível*

Further Reading

On the PT
In English:
Margaret Keck, *The Workers' Party and Democratization in Brazil*, Yale University Press, New Haven, 1992

Emir Sader and Ken Silverstein, *Without Fear of Being Happy: Lula, the Workers Party and Brazil*, Verso, London, 1991

In Portuguese:
Fernando Gabeira et al, *Viagem ao coraçao do Brasil*, Editora Página Aberta, São Paulo, 1994

Marta Harnecker, *O Sonho era Possível*, MEPLA/Casa América Livre, São Paulo, 1994

On Brazil
Sue Branford & Oriel Glock, *The Last Frontier: Fighting Over Land in the Amazon*, Zed Books, London, 1985

Caipora Women's Group, *Women in Brazil*, Latin America Bureau, London, 1993

Kevin Danaher and Michael Shellenberger (eds), *Fighting for the Soul of Brazil*, Monthly Review Press, New York, 1993

Gilberto Dimenstein, *Brazil: War on Children*, Latin America Bureau, London, 1991

Lúcio Kowarick (ed), *Social Struggles in the City: The Case of São Paulo*, Monthly Review Press, New York, 1994

Carolina Maria de Jesus, *Beyond All Pity: The Diary of Carolina Maria de Jesus*, Earthscan Publications, London, 1990

Chico Mendes, *Fight for the Forest: Chico Mendes in His Own Words*, Latin America Bureau, London, 1992

Thomas E Skidmore, *Black into White: Race and Nationality in Brazilian Thought*, Duke University Press, Durham, North Carolina, 1993

Organisations working on Brazil in the UK

Action Brazil
26A Chatsworth Road, London NW2 4BS
Promotes the 'Campaign Against Hunger in Brazil', raising funds and sending second-hand clothes to Brazil.

Brazil Network
PO Box 1325, London SW9 0RA
Links individuals and organisations working on Brazil and interested in keeping up to date on events there. Publishes a quarterly newsletter.

Brazilian Arts and Community Centre
1 Elgin Avenue, London W9
Provides a range of services for the Brazilian community.

Brazilian Contemporary Arts
Palingswick House, 241 King St, London W6 9LP
Organises cultural events and publishes regular newsletter.

Brazilian Embassy
32 Green St, London W1Y 4AT

Leros
25A Collingbourne Rd, London W12 0SG
Free Portuguese-language magazine for the Brazilian community in Britain.

PT
PO Box 3698, London SW2 1XB
Contact for its London branch. Organises events, fund-raisers etc.

Task Brasil
140 Bermondsey Street, London SE1 3TX
New organisation, planning to set up a network of shelters for street children in Brazil.

Organisations working on Brazil in North America

Brazil Information Committee
c/o Global Exchange, 2017 Mission St, #303, San Francisco CA 94110
Sells a video about the PT, 'Without Fear of Being Happy'.

Brazil Action Solidarity Exchange (BASE)
c/o Global Exchange (address as above)
Publishes a monthly newsletter

Amaaka'a Amazon Network
339 Lafayette St, New York, NY 10003

UTOPIA UNARMED
The Latin American Left After the Cold War
Jorge G. Castañeda

Extraordinary....[This book] attempts to do nothing less than restore direction to the Latin American left...Surprising and refreshing.' **Los Angeles Times**

Castro's Cuba is isolated; the guerrillas who once spread havoc through Argentina and Uruguay are dead, dispersed or running for office as moderates. And in 1990, Nicaragua's Sandinistas were rejected at the polls by their own constituents.

Are these symptoms of the fall of the Latin American left? Or are they merely temporary lulls in an ongoing revolution that may yet transform the hemisphere?

In **Utopia Unarmed**, Jorge Castañeda tells the story behind the failed movements of the past thirty years. But he also suggests that the left has a continuing relevance in a continent that suffers from ever-increasing destitution and social inequality, and proposes a new left political agenda for the region. **Utopia Unarmed** combines insiders' accounts of intrigue and armed struggle with a clear-sighted analysis of the mechanisms of day-to-day power.

'Utopia Unarmed is a timely contribution ... a devastating critique [by] a leading particiant in amny of the events which are narrated here ... of the Latin American left from within - courageous and unsentimental, admirably free of cant, euphemism and evasion.' **Times Literary Supplement**

Jorge Castañeda is professor of economics and international affairs at the National Autonomous University of Mexico.

489 pages, index, 1995 ISBN 0-679-75141-6 (pbk) £14.00

Published in North America by Vintage Books

Exclusive distribution in the UK and British Commonwealth by the Latin America Bureau

THE LATIN AMERICAN LEFT
From the Fall of Allende to Perestroika
Barry Carr & Steve Ellner (eds)

With the collapse of the eastern bloc and the rise of neoliberalism, the Left appears increasingly isolated in many parts of the world. In Latin America, however, despite Cuba's economic crisis and the disintegration of orthodox communism, the Left has emerged from decades of dictatorship and repression with new identities and forms of participation.

In eight country studies, contributors examine the failure of the 1960s guerrilla strategies, the challenge posed by the new social movements and the new emphasis on democratic reforms over socioeconomic change. Looking at the erosion of US influence in Latin America and the social impact of structural adjustment policies, the book also explores regional issues such as trade union struggles and guerrilla warfare.

Chapters cover the situation in Chile, Peru, Colombia, Mexico, El Salvador, Bolivia, Venezuela, Argentina and Brazil.

'A timely publication which will commend itself to students coming to grips with political developments in the region, and to those who remember where they were on the day that Allende fell from power.'
Society for Latin American Studies Newsletter

256 pages, index, 1993   ISBN 0 906156 72 6 (pbk)   £14.00

Published in North America by Westview Press

Prices are for paperback editions and include postage and packing.

LAB books are available by post from Latin America Bureau, 1 Amwell Street, London EC1R 1UL. Cheques payable to LAB. Write for a free catalogue.